MARK IN TIME

PORTRAITS & POETRY / SAN FRANCISCO

PHOTOGRAPHER: CHRISTA FLEISCHMANN   COORDINATOR: ROBERT E. JOHNSON

EDITOR: NICK HARVEY   PUBLISHER: GLIDE PUBLICATIONS, SAN FRANCISCO

This work is part of an on-going collection of portraiture and poetry begun in December 1968 by photographer Christa Fleischmann and Robert E. Johnson, then Director of Intersection, an interdenominational center for religion and the arts in San Francisco. *Mark in Time* is published for Intersection by Glide Publications as part of its program of presenting to the world strong statements of religious value. Poetry, like all art, challenges us from a deeper level of reality to re-evaluate ourselves and be open to change, to new life.

We are grateful to all the poets in this volume for their generosity and understanding in making this work possible. In addition, the editor would like to thank all those who helped in reaching poets: Beverly Dahlen of The Poetry Center at San Francisco State College, Eleanor Sully of KPFA, Dave Cole, Jim Wehlage, Michael Nagler, Edith Kramer, J. J. Wilson, and Peter Bailey; and, for their patience, his co-workers in bringing this collection into published form.

In almost all cases, the work included in this volume represents the poet's own choice. Our intent has been to let each poet speak directly, with a minimum of editorial intrusion.

The following poems have appeared elsewhere:

"David," in *Poems 1930–1960* by Josephine Miles. Copyright © 1960 by Indiana University Press. Reprinted by permission of Josephine Miles and Indiana University Press.

"The Prestidigitator," by Al Young, in *Brilliant Corners;* used with permission.

"A Dry Day Just Before the Rainy Season," in *The Back Country* by Gary Snyder. Copyright © 1968 by Gary Snyder. Reprinted by permission of New Directions Publishing Corporation.

"Egyptian Book of the Dead," in the book *De Mayor of Harlem,* by David Henderson; copyright © 1965, 1967, 1969, 1970 by David Henderson. Published by E. P. Dutton & Co., Inc., and reprinted with their permission.

'Lines for a Fifty-fifth Birthday," by Jeanne McGahey, in *Works* quarterly; used with permission of Jeanne McGahey and the editors of *Works.*

"Salute!", by Lawrence Ferlinghetti, in *Ramparts* magazine; used with permission of the author.

"Come," in *Golden Sardine* by Bob Kaufman; copyright © 1967 by Bob Kaufman. Reprinted by permission of City Lights Books.

"Discovering the Pacific," by Thom Gunn, in *Poetry* (Chicago); used with permission of the author.

"clumsy with," by Jeannetta Jones, in *Caterpiller No. 10;* used with permission of the author.

"The photo," in *Moments of Doubt* by Lennart Bruce. Copyright © 1969 by Cloud Marauder Press, and reprinted with their permission.

"It is difficult . . .", in *Of Being Numerous* by George Oppen. Copyright © 1968 by George Oppen. Reprinted by permission of New Directions Publishing Corporation.

"The Number One Daughter of the Wang Family," in *Why I Live on the Mountain,* by C. H. Kwock and Vincent McHugh; used by permission of C. H. Kwock.

"Yin and Yang," in *Collected Shorter Poems* by Kenneth Rexroth. Copyright © 1966 by Kenneth Rexroth. Reprinted by permission of New Directions Publishing Corporation.

"Six Reveilles to Match My Self-Indulgence," by Wilder Bentley, is part of a much longer sequence of sonnets, sestinas, and a *canzone* entitled "According to the Wisdom of an Angel".

"The Diamond," by Daniel Moore, is part of a longer sequence entitled "States of Amazement."

"The Passport" in *The Mechanic* by Luis Garcia. © 1970 by Luis Garcia. Used with permission.

"Ascent," by Lynn Strongin, in *Manroot* magazine; used with permission.

"Shaman Songs 12" in *Shaman Songs* by Gene Fowler. © for the author by dustbooks, 1966; used with permission.

Library of Congress catalog card number: 70-141852
International Standard Book Number: 0-912078-16-2
Manufactured in the U.S.A. by Fortune House, San Francisco

MARK IN TIME

For her special assistance, I wish to thank Miss Almut Hellmann, a young photographer, who has aided and encouraged me throughout a long and arduous assignment.

I am also indebted to Mr. Robert E. Johnson who originally discussed the book with me; not only for his gracious co-operation and assistance, but for his personal interest.

Acknowledgment must go to the Glide Urban Center for making the publication of this book possible.

In humble appreciation, I wish to dedicate the book to all poets, everywhere.

Christa Fleischmann

Foreword

No strictly local terms or national boundaries can ever define the involved and interdependent influences of creative minds. Yet, works of imagination seem always to spring from the specific impulses of place and time.

This book presents the varied faces and works of 80 poets, who have, for different reasons and various lengths of time, been described as belonging to or associated with the San Francisco community of poets.

The aim of the book is to offer a large number of representative works, the majority of them new and unpublished, by the most diverse yet best of poets.

We do not claim that the collection is definitive or comprehensive. It is a mark in time — one which we hope will not only bring the reader into a closer understanding and appreciation of the poets herein, but will be an effective advertisement for the best poetry of all kinds.

Contents

David

Goliath stood up clear in the assumption of status,
Strong and unquestioning of himself and others,
Fully determined by the limits of his experience.
I have seen such a one among surgeons, sergeants,
Deans, and giants, the power implicit.

Then there was David, who made few assumptions,
Had little experience, but for more was ready,
Testing and trying this pebble or that pebble,
This giant or that giant.
He is not infrequent.

How could Goliath guess, with his many assumptions,
The force of the slung shot of the pure-hearted?
How could David fear, with his few hypotheses,
The power of status which is but two-footed?
So he shot, and shouted!

JOSEPHINE MILES

The Prestidigitator

A prestidigitator makes things disappear,
vanish, not unlike a well-paid bookkeeper
or tax consultant or champion consumer

The poet is a prestidigitator, he makes
your old skins disappear & re-clothes you
in sturdy raiment of thought, feeling, soul,

dream & happenstance. Consider him villain of
the earthbound, a two-fisted cowboy with
pencil in one hand & eraser in the other

dotting the horizon of your heart with cool
imaginary trees but rubbing out more than he
leaves in for space so light can get thru

AL YOUNG

Wingwalking in Oregon

Last Sunday petrified
on Bridal Veil, a beginner's climb,
trail no wider than a carton of Kents.
Nice cliff & Eiffel view
for families
fresh from church. But
goosed by heights, how can I
embrace the sublime
without a priest
& no goddam fence?

And now
Saddle Mountain,
called benign.
Trail this time
half a loaf of bread
& the scenery true
until I find
I'm looking over the edge
of Oregon
into the depths of Idaho
& think of potatoes, breadcrumbs, birds
& diseases of birds, starch in the blood,
playground donkeys, slides, songs
& other conveyances
of my childhood
& if somehow
I let go
& spider down
concentrated & green
what should I, if alive but above all
safe, remember, & to whom
will I complain?

ROBERT PETERSON

for greed. & human smallnes
s became history. Would you
? To commence slaughter? No
contact of other. Diary was
something when we tilt the
museum. Try you can't use t
o listen. Less worries or w
ind about my travel. It is
arriving. Small he fold up
not to rattle. Are you nece
ssary again? Hotel painted
in live tales. Izzie told w
hat was meant. The inferenc
e was quite convinging. WWI
and all that. Tiburon Hills
Or just plain Russia, Joe..
Fast Bill, for heaven's ake
Stalin's heavy camouflage..
To travel M dilations?Trist
e. Agonies in Harwick. So d
im this recent war where Ik
e plays Hitler with dust. D
oes not possess ocean pictu
res. A cigarette pose to la
y off electric. For Ano....
Had it been with relevance
it might have happened. Put
away with no exception. The
y obeyed remote Sunday like
children of the Jews. On th
eir right after the gun. In
tellectuals are crying my p
arrot already? Stein's out
there. A bank is burned? Th
e Panzers fold up against y
ou. Radioactive image junk
vision invades the old crot
ch. Dining time of streets
once before. Simultaneous c
alendars in low black betra
yals. Dead stars already ru
n the air. Crushed contacts
latch the system which said
that. Best Connecticut sile
nce in dirty. & form it you
say? My ducksoup. So now to
y pistols. Inferred quite s
oldiers put away thorough.
Their bellies in flame coll
ecting comatose envoys. Ut!
They made the studio hall.
& out of showbiz..money on
the war. Did you? From Ray?
Mar in soft liked Ferrarri.
Let's stop for Tina's machi
ne accord. Russia the Mayan
priest. Is now to the ally.
A telephone army has sailed
for other Adolph. "Gun it V
ance for south africal" The
ir car might. Thor sped on
to know for such a cigarett
e. In wind form it. Their c
ountry has tunnels of mean
pigs. Allies show up halluc
inating contacts. Look at H
err Doktor Anyplace & other
nonmembers. Constipated my
point? Our man shrieks the
bible? Interest to trail fa
st. Ike rolled a cigarette
hello from Apo. Senile tele

JAN HERMAN

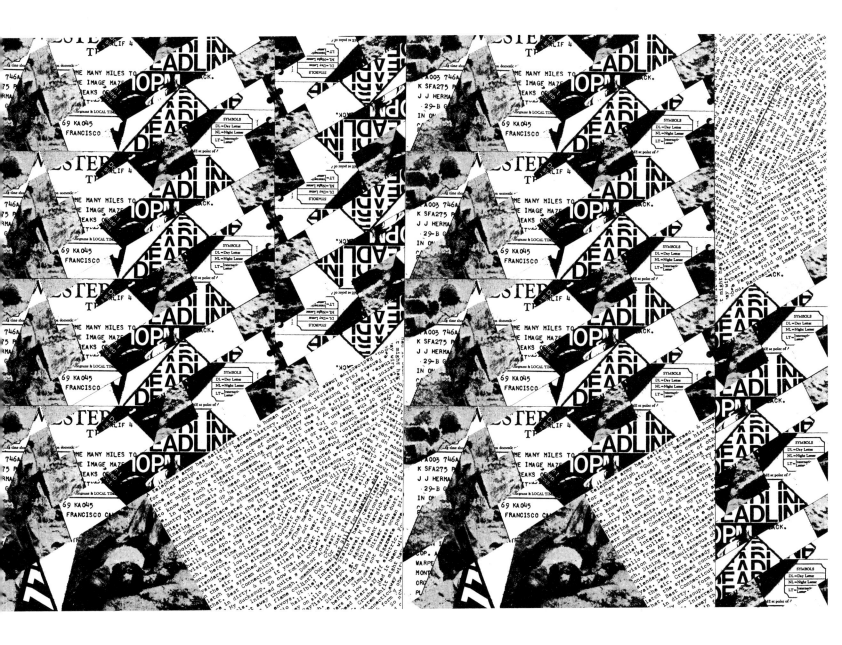

Lines on the Back of a Leary Bailfund Card

there is a time of notation
on the body / body of words
for which we are not fully
responsible   the pattern
not of choosing / where-to-go
takes us into itself
no escape willing

to endure its self this part
of place is me / you say
and to what do we belong
be long in a place is to
be possessed by what energy
we give to it and the body
bears little weight in the
matter / what's the matter

you say / is mind over-
taken by embracing
only that careful closure
within the walls of our
hands / I love you and
I weep that music

makes my way through
the channels of
your mind to know
I have no place
yet needing to place that
which is yours to give
willful to the time

MARY NORBERT KÖRTE

Forte: for Tina

Not the divine rising up from earth as dew
turned to steam by sunlight.
Not the divine going to Paradise on shimmering escalators.
I want the divine without contrivance.
No image or dance to prepare me for it.
There are enough distractions.

•

The fire of holy letters burns thru stone.
No need to fear pain light tears from you.

•

All sacred texts as simple as
bringing the flesh together in love.

•

You must have your earth & bring forth from it
a life harvest of children
who carry on the rising up.
I must have my space between heaven & earth
& count beads & listen to the laughter of angels
who celebrate all our good works.

•

DAVID MELTZER

From *Six Reveilles to Match My Self=Indulgence*

4

Up, up, old Benedict, the bard who would
Outnumber laureate Petrarch's leaves to Laura —
Outleaf the *Manyoshu,* if he but could —
Continuing frustration, a plethora
Of desire, but adding fat to fire his *should!*
No humanist with higher learning's aura,
Inspired at court, bemused by solitude,
Art thou, whose grudging celibacy's been more a
Trial than tribute to thy hardihood.

Yet humanist or no, there is no way
To weasel out of Love's indenturement —
No writ of manumission save sustained
Philandering in sonnet form! — Lo, till Love's Day
Of Judgment free thee from thy daily stint
Of dunlinsong, bemoan Love's numbered sand!

WILDER BENTLEY

Yolanthe

Yolanthe
        (secretly named
Sings
By the side of a silver stream
In moonlight corporeal as
A fat body; swells the night.

Yolanthe
        (unacknowledged
Prays
Among the silver willows
Hearing the woolen voice of the owl
Drawn like a shawl across the stars.

Yolanthe
        (long sought
Weeps
Under the beating wing of
The night hawk; shivering
White against the brigand fog.

Yolanthe
        (disguised
Dies
Silently sinking under
Weightless mists, the false rain;
And the sham light.

Yolanthe
        (whose song is unheard

DAN KENNEY

The Golden Witch

When I was wed
I took a golden witch to bed
and she turned sheets to lightning
falling, and led me through
her eyes to a thousand
bright deaths.
And other things she did.
She turned birds to china
in the air,
and wore their
shattered bodies
in her hair.
Honey
Blood
Salt
Amber
Silver
Fire.

ALAN DIENSTAG

Ascent

I cannot live
without rapture.
Fashion me a house of compassion.

Carpenter, along the scaffold
I walk in bloody twilight.
My toes grip the boards.

I am seeking
out
my beloved.

The ladder has been
removed:
Solitary on the skeleton

I stand.
Only archangels
beyond.

———

Kid, twelve,
tormented
thy friend

will creep back
sheepishly,
set the ladder on the sill

and leave you place
to descend: First the slender feet
grip

the ladder;
then thy cold palms,
the upper rungs.

As you gaze
at the house you climbed
in the dirt field

it's twilight.
Peace. The earth is cold.
The covenant is sealed.

LYNN STRONGIN

A Dry Day Just Before the Rainy Season

DRUNK last night
    drunk the night before

talking and shouting and laughing, maybe
I should've been home reading —
"all right *don't* leave me alone —
    do something with me then!"
            the landlady's son
heard through a back wall window.

Sunday morning, november, plenty of birds
a pair of red-shafted flickers
        on the peach tree
    stretch wings
      showing the white-flash back
      linnets crack seeds at the feed tray.

Not too hung over —
I suppose I'll get drunk tonight.
one year: from rain to wistaria,
apricot blossoms, all night singing,
     sleeping on the floor,
off to work in the Sierra
     back in august
    cool fog, dryness,
leaves on the fruit trees fall.

Soon the rain starts again.
smell of burning leaves,
orange berries, red berries a
      sudden jump cat
        — I know him —
bee rattles in a flower
    this warm sober day

I wonder what I said to everybody

GARY SNYDER

'The lake
                'is not encumbered by the swan'
   the rose
             no great weight to the stem
If therefore I am borne
                   beyond time
   to an interim
              where women and men
dispose of the world
            free
according to the beat
              of their blood
ungovernably whirled
                in the centrifuge love
then
      let rose and world
                answer your look
you! reason and rhyme
              and the whole book
of being
          whereby creatures and gods
inhabit the swan
            and see
in the unmoving lake
              their cool
images dissolve
           each
making
         a moody paradigm
of the other
           and resolve

into the swan again
                —the one swan
bold
       and changeable
              as the dawn

VINCENT McHUGH

Short Pastoral

Three-days rain and
Right in the middle of town
This small farmhouse.
                    I could have
Dressed, rushed out, come back
In five minutes with a wild
Armful of wet apples
Or one warm egg
For a love gift.
                    Freud
Was out in the barn
Munching hay with Marx,
And Darwin dozed in the loft.

We were alone for miles
With honest coffee
And a few words. You said:
I'd sure hate to live in town.
I said: This farming —
It won't pay.

LEONARD NATHAN

One Fragment for God

I give praise to thee God for thy kingfisher creeks
And thy tributary freshets throbbing the sources of streams.
I give praise to thee for the hauteur of high rivers going West.
I give praise for the harmony of lakes,
The dapple of shallows and eddies,
The quietude of water forever at peace with itself,
The mirrors of stillness.
I give praise to thee for the love sound of ripples at night,
And the sucking theft sound at noon,
The cat-glide creek under the east, the dawn hush.
And for muteness, the surd
Inferential music. These meanings, the essences
Of fern, moss, this secrecy and wonder,
Thy startling wet . . .

WILLIAM EVERSON

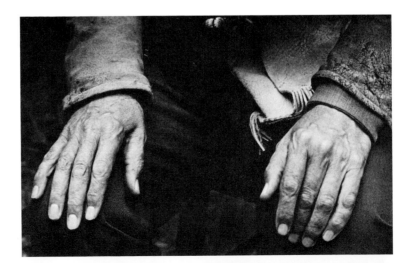

38

Beginning Again As Morning

Your bones left out all night
gathering secrets from the grass
have become more simple now,
and the daylight enters them
with the wind as midwife,
carving a date
in the marble of your cheek —
I think they have said
quit walking around with a grave
on your shoulder. It's not worth
the weight of a log.
Kneel down with the insects
where the sea has been folding
a scarf for you,
open her leaves of water.

God

After waking I look down across our bodies —
He is this search I have to make each morning
for my hands — like any form of blindness.

EUGENE RUGGLES

The Knight of the Sad Face

¡Y Dios no te de paz si gloria!
  Miguel de Unamuno

Treating of songs
              In a wild wood plain
Infested with twirling sprigs of sky-tearing mills
A figure indulging age and a cavern mind
Speared the sun smearing his lance with light.
And a soiled sky lit a cigarette star
To guide a warrior to his washing.
   If a truth were to happen,
   A song born
   To some decisive year
Promising bread and fishes
      One was not sure would multiply
Would the uncertain glory of an acute wound
Pay the price of spilling peace
      Into a fouled net of undertaking?
High daring walks on spindly legs
And stars too often are the cause of death.

Golden Gate

Hay otros puentes —
   grises y duros
   que abarcan las heridas de los cerros
               sangrando ríos color de hiel —
pero no como esta telaraña anaranjada
que pierde sus hilos en las nubes de acero
y gime levemente
   como si tuviera una estrella entre dientes.
      — Hay otros puentes
      — otras bahías
donde bebe el sol
y la sal se engendra —
      pero en este los rezos como moscas cautivas
      esperan que baje de su nido de plomo
la araña del tiempo
con malicia en el vientre
   que vigila siempre
   la avenida del puente.

RAFAEL JESÚS GONZÁLEZ

Egyptian Book of the Dead

pharisees come bloom
water eddys the twilight air
blue for music
red for fire
look out along the rooftops
ancient cities pop up
old testaments
tribes muster at grey street corners
sparks of cigarettes gleam the glass arcades
wine bottles libate the sidewalk
no more
the wine from palms
no more
the beer from bananas
but
easy now
easy
this night will turn you on/

where
death is a beautiful thing
done in the right way
and to die
tonight
in the street
on the radio
in the fire
will fare us well

we who are nothing
to the incarnate computers
save factors on a graph
we who are nothing
rescued by love
we cannot fathom
walk jaded neon jewelry

twinkling
twinkling
so delicate to the touch
to fall down
in a blaze of trumpets
in a blossom of fire
we
are from a place far off

DAVID HENDERSON

Baltimore Eclipse

Did you see the sun blotted from sky
like when the world ends and your hands
get cold and old women look witchy
and tell you strange tales. . . .
Did you see strangers arrive in the
field of straw and ice to warn
you of the theft of the sun.
And who's that skawking with an idiot grin?
Who's that and that and that who have no
feathers or shadows when evening was
two in the afternoon. (Total over
Virginia Beach and Edgar Cayce . . .)
I saw the ashes of my sister through
cobalt of the black sun. I felt the ozone change.
I saw the door of eternity creak open, creak
open from that peakhole into time.
Who may have crouched there
crouched there before . . .
unawares of cosmic superimposition.
Who was caught there
was caught there now, in the phantom's solid stare
Oh God I did not see this sneak preview
of things to come

lost in the garden of remembrance
when the young walked without gravity
where guards were stripped of their armory.
I saw the fairy tale stare painted in
the doll's eyes of the wired man,
flashing blue, flashing blue,
wired eels swimming through the aether
and grey lads from Beatle movies,
this street is an aquarium
with all types of fishes swimming 'round.
A newsboy just clipped me for a fin.
But oh what sheen, this dust of gold,
the crisp acetelyne evening
the city washed with purple ozone.
The hour Poe arose from his statue
and strolled around, I saw him musty & grey,
hair ragged, falling to shoulder,
he acknowledged his fellow statues
admiring their wings and horses.
He strolled down the hill
to get in his statue.
Over his shoulder, looking, looking.

CHARLES PLYMELL

For Kenneth Patchen

Some people are born
to walk through pain
as if it were their own.
Their shoes walk empty
    with shadows in them
    shadows filled with sweat
        a hint of glass
          an undiscernable size
        a mob of paper
         insulating the soul
       the grains of a hard wood
    held together with leather where
the nails have gone in.

A certain cobbler
works late into the night
making shoes for these ghosts
    each strike of his hammer
       nailing a name
         to a hollow in our throats.

WAYNE MILLER

Lines for a Fifty-fifth Birthday

I stopped the doctor busy with his hemps;
I called him from his wounding. Sir, I cried,
(And caught the small bright muscle of his eye)
Bring halters, poultices: the several inhabitants
Of the body, the unspeakable organs, they falter,
The greases drain away: and the stone forms in the bile
like a bitter jewel, and the luck is out.

The goat said long ago, the lion said,
King's X, this would not happen:
And a voice far off:
Any spirit involved among these tendons
Like a jugged hare in a pot
It has only to speak.

But the years arriving
Were not informed. Here came the pages tattling;
Here came the postman stamping like half a horse,
And I, poor animal, not ringed about with unicorns
Or any doves to flap
Like a Monday wash,
Now in the wind from that most ungainly north
So stand and stiffen.

Deformity neither scarred nor blessed:
Forsworn, but not foreseen.

JEANNE McGAHEY

Tides

It will darken, stars glimmering, repeating —
                    the vast tide
spinning us into it,
                involving us deftly
in the terms of your defeat,

   in the darkness that is cracking
                    like a portrait,
   living and beating like a scar —

   rejecting, like a sparrow,
               what is given,
     the answers you provoke, and control
             in your careful errors,
     in the electricity of your rigid room
     where you burn like a heretic.

The skull, that bone, tight and luminous
               with the pressure of speech,
       unlocks.

With pointed hands you separate the bones
     from an uncontrollable past.
It is stained, truculent,
and fabrics of the stiff light hang
     from the twisted brackets.

This is the completion you supposed
of the heart's luminous, loud and bleeding heel.

     The coast dismantles
     and shines long after. . . .
     And the heavens change like amethyst
       among the white, implacable stars.

FRED OSTRANDER

After the Storm

Along the streaming ground, the wet leaves
          fit like fish
And shine like talk.
The prints of the xylophone horses
Clang and revise
Their clear and candid marks.

And only a funeral under a tall quartz sky
Can bring us together as steeply
As these oak trees
And this tomb.

All talk seems genuine: the syllables make evident
Their wild, pronounced colonies.

The word is out — a racket of hail and rhyme
Is landing a few Greek letters at a time.

If any have other knowledge of the crime,
Let him speak, lest the privilege harden;
Let us acknowledge
The rains were heavy and the damage severe —

Yet there are times when the uncut universe comes close
And whets like a diamond;

And the diamond is odd in its meaning;
It rests in its water-mark;
Is read by the shining door:

That the privacy of clarity emerge,
and the useful joy seem near.

ROSALIE MOORE BROWN

Land's End

Not just one night, but all the nights
I've wandered here, stirring birds and
Counting waves, while the sunny moon
Kept burning holes in thoughts
I'd saved for darkened walks.

Squat ships of steel surprise
By standing on the nervous sea
As though their hearts were cork
Concealed in livid shawls
To tease the staring shore.

The late straw grasses of a
Dry season litter earth turned
Old with waiting, while torn trees
Turn from the gone sea wind
In living fear of its return.

Implacable as litanies
The night-time water comes
To slide its seamless hands
Across the gray and sandy
Belly of its solitary love.

Deep in a catacombed cove where
Even fools would dread the dead
Birds lie, too damp for ants, un-
Turned sand about their marbled
Eyes as though some more could happen.

Here, on the tapering brink
That ends my home, the cathedral
Size of nature weights
The soul with endlessness
Until the cries of children

Tearing new flowers from
Their earth would seem
A peace against the terror
Of this land too long too
Close to the overwhelming sea.

DANIEL J. LANGTON

JEFF BERNER

What Holds the Universe Together

Everything is stuck together
everything sticks and sticks together
   and we stick to it
   and we're stuck in it
we're part of the sticky too.

Everything is stuck together
everything sticks in the muck together
   and we're thick in it
   we're mucked up in it
we're stuck with Original Glue.

Everything is stuck together
everything sticks in a gooey structure
   and we're stuck to it
   and we're stuck with it
we're all in God's structured goo.

JAMES BROUGHTON

Vita-Sheet

tip-burning wings
put out the fire   finally
to make charcoal calligraphy
valid
easily smudged
but fingerprint-true

eyes sting memory
murine or some other such damn product
clear
long enough to put the story down
in some tangible form

a garbage-truck somewhere always
a washed-down sidewalk early morning
slippery
this is the city
i have been born into
any city
the city

yearning for air
for greenfor the tree
i embrace
the city
still
as a halt
faltering step
one foot in front
of the other
gouging cement the foot seeks green

imprint intangible
on cement hostile
yet taking it all in
all in
the aeons of footprint
do carry the message

A HUMAN UPON THIS STRANGE
INEVITABLE STRUCTURE
the city

RUTH WEISS

The Song Mt. Tamalpais Sings

This is the last place, there is nowhere else to go

>   Human movements,
>   but for a very few,
>   are Westerly.

>   Man follows the Sun.

This is the last place, there is nowhere else to go

>   Or follows what he thinks to be
>   the movement of the Sun.
>   it is hard to feel it as a rider
>   on a spinning ball.

This is the last place, there is nowhere else to go

>   Centuries and hordes of us
>   from every quarter of the earth
>   now piling up
>   and each wave going back to get some more

This is the last place, there is nowhere else to go

>   "My face is the map of the Steppes" she said,
>   on this mountain, looking West.

>   My blood set singing by it
>   to the old tunes
>   Irish
>   among these oaks

This is the last place, there is nowhere else to go

>   Now we shall celebrate the great spring tides
>   Beaches are strewn again with
>   agate, jasper, and jade.
>   The mussel-rocks stand clear.

This is the last place, there is nowhere else to go

>   Now let us celebrate the
>   headland's huge
>   cairn-studded fall into the sea

This is the last place, there is nowhere else to go

>   For we have walked the jeweled beaches
>   at the feet of the final cliffs
>   of all Man's wanderings

This is the last place

>   *There is nowhere else we need to go*

LEW WELCH

64

IT IS NOT YOUTH THAT INTRIGUES ME BUT SUPPLENESS.
The sensitivity of meat to meat and to nerve
dies with the nets of self-image.
THE SELF BECOMES RIGID
and does not open
AND EXTEND.
The structure
is frozen and rusts
like armor. Spring comes
and goes
with buds and creatures.

WE LOOK INTO A VISION
and only see
it narrowing. Beyond
that
there is a mystery
in this life like a candle flame
AND

it is moving.

I would be as perfect as a moth.

MICHAEL McCLURE

Misa Mayor

Eres lo que eres
cuando en tí reflejas tu pensamiento entero.
Mas cuando otro intentas imitar, confuso . . .
mueres.
Eres lo que eres.
No importa que a veces nos sintamos vacíos,
como casas deshabitadas
porque todo es a veces.
¿Quiénes somos nosotros
que nunca satisfechos con trivialidades,
caminamos con el tiempo
y morimos con prequntas?
Nosotros somos los sencillos
que cantamos arrogantes
y que mientras reímos,
un silbido suena hueco
en el centro de nosotros mismos.
Es un sonido triste
que rasgando las entrañas
nos eleva a las cumbres
y que luego, arriba, se esparce
y revolotea por el aire.
Eres lo que eres.
Y vaya, quién dijera
la vida es la verdadera voz de la tristeza;
la dulce y vinatérica voz, suava catapulta
que lanza a aquél a la agonía;
la vida siembra la cosecha de nosotros mismos;
de lo que somos, lo que sentimos, ¡Ay!
y vemos: la mismísima tristeza,
Pero vente.
Ven conmigo. La tristeza también tiene su cara buena,

A la hora de la Misa Mayor,
silencio, silencio,
que es hora de la hostia espiritual.
Mil cosas se escabullen en el filo de esta noche,
y el alba incaica, azteca y maya llega.
Eres lo que eres.

AMÍLCAR LOBOS

Between the Electric Rhythm and the Melodic Mind

The yearner for silence, believing in the quiet mind,
Is forced to a recognition of noise
When vibrating music hooks the world
With jolting sound — "orgasmic grunts, tortured squeals,
Lascivious moans, electric disasters . . . It eats you alive."
At an airport, the whining blast of jet planes
Sears the sky with fiery, white paths . . .
I imagine Saint Francis bouncing along
These white trails in the sky, bare feet dangling,
Bells jingling from his ankles, softly,
To warn the crickets safely away from his noisy passage . . .
Do not hear this as a plea for quietude of soul.
Watch on the shore how high waves smash the beach,
How noise finds its silence on the sand,
Moving between electric rhythm and the melodic mind.

JAMES SCHEVILL

To a Proud Old Woman Watching the Tearing Down of the Hurricane Shed

You did not see wood made pliable my rot, or rust-devoured iron,
Or rain-gutter riddled like a cabbage-leaf. No, none of these
Not jagged flowerpot, or tile without echo, table without leg, or chair bereft
Of arms you saw, or planks striped like a zebra's hide
With mold. Each board they fed the flame, bepearled with writhing slug,
Woven with worm, remained sweet timber of another year,
Wine-sapped with memory, crowned with lacy green, ripped,
Slugless and rotless, from out the static of your history.

(You saw in the old shed's dying your youth die, mourned only
By the turtle-doves this spring. The child and girl and woman named Felicity,
Writhed by the strong sea-wall in separate agony; the breasts, limbs, lovely cranium of all you were
Consumed at last, and through clenched teeth you cried your hideous name.
Yours were the entrails twisting in the flame, the soul dragged, screaming,
From the shed's black rot, ash dow with the dust of woems not written,
Grace not said, ash with the long decay of all you were to be, and were not.
This was a lynching of the past you could not countenance, that brought you to your knees
Under the pale tears of the dogwood's drifting leaves.)

But there have been other lynchings, fiercer, bloodier. There have been more savage dramas played,
The rope of terror tightening on the throat, the neck jerked, broken,
Like the heart, and your hand nor any other lifted, and no requiem sung.
Think now of these others, now that the last bleached ember of the shed is gone. Oh, not for long
Does the high wind of our life take all we speak
From out our mouths, to bear it loudly, clearly, down the air
So that the living and the dead may hear.

(Let it be courage that our tongues compose,
There being no refuge from the hurricane that blows.)

KAY BOYLE

Al Capone in Alaska

or
hoodoo ecology vs the judeo-
christian tendency to *let em
have it!*

The Eskimo hunts
the whale & each year
the whale flowers for the
Eskimo.
This must be love baby!
One receiving with respect
from a Giver who has
plenty.
There is no hatred here.
There is One Big Happy
Family here.

American & Canadian Christians
submachine gun the whales.
They gallantly sail out &
shoot them as if the Pacific
were a Chicago garage on
St. Valentine's day

ISHMAEL REED

NORMAN OGUE MUSTILL

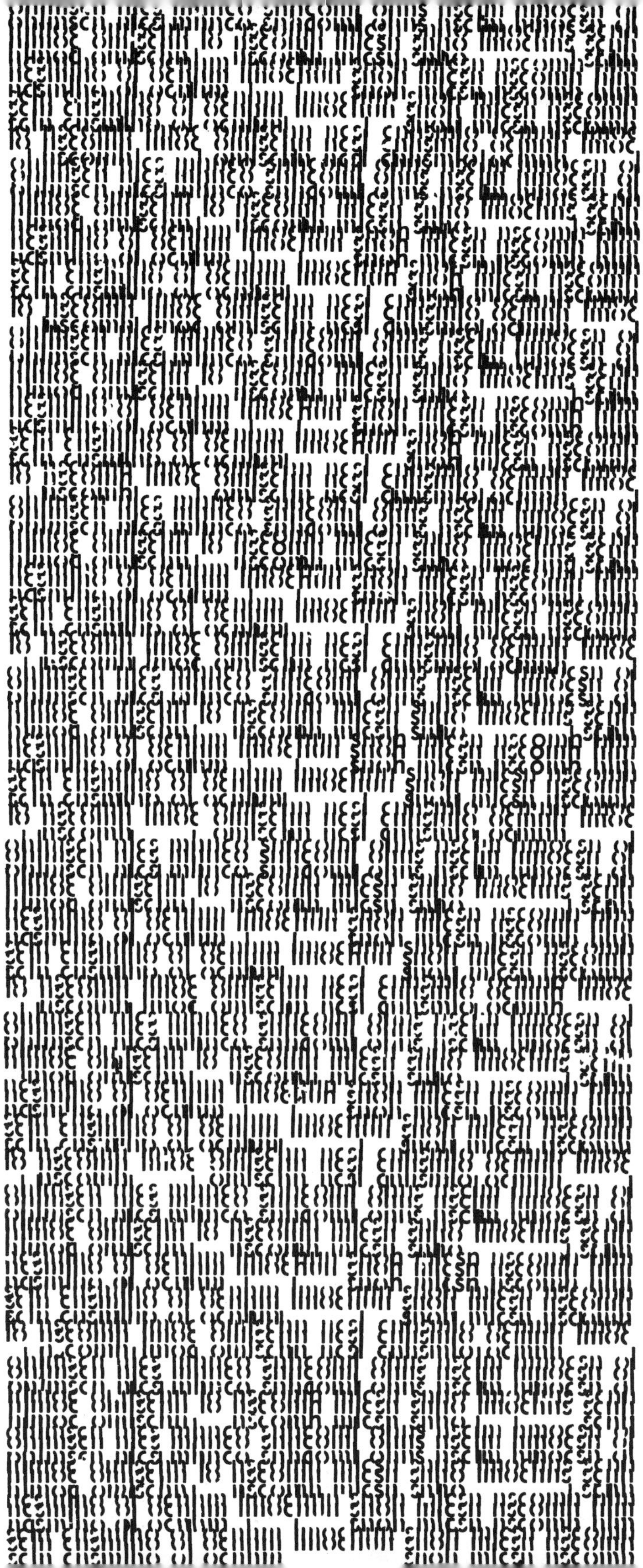

From *Birds of Hazard and Prey*

With great difficulty I managed to get out of my skin
After some hair-raising moments everything goes smoothly
My arm is now fully disengaged and I lift myself literally
Out of myself by deftly inserting my liberated finger
Between my shoulder and the lining beneath the muscle
I pull and push and slowly but surely it slides out
The opening is now big enough for the head
A quick tug is all it takes and I am out
What an amazing purity of consciousness
What an experience to see the world
Without the self's enveloping atmosphere
Everything is trembling with transparent colour
Women's thoughts are readable as the daily paper
The minds of little children contain untold marvels
The men magnificent like painted savages
The trees a patch of liquid green flowing
Into the earth's hands holding the sky's vessel
I am now squeezing the rest of me out
At last I am free of myself as I have never been before
Now I can see who was this other me I heard so much about
A pure structure of thoughts sensations and emotions
Built inside a body of words with intervals
As vast as the stars of a galaxy
Against the blackness of eternal silence.

NANOS VALAORITIS

Forgive?

In the cold compassion
Of my bosom
Habrá perdón
For
My destructors?

To find warmth
In
A
Corazón
Hard-frozen—

When the thaws of
Primaveras have
Come and have gone
    Sería imposible—

Wouldn't one's
Uneasy adversary
    think the same
    heridas that
    expose the heart
    of the heart
    would . . .

Surely welcome
El calordelos
Rayos—rays of
Warmth, however
Sparse?
    Wouldn't he?

Indeed, si el acero
Which pierces deja
Una funda que repela
El calór

. . . sealing hurts
forever. Y las
recompensas se vuelven
las red hot scars

That defy the time-healing-time
That fails, and so, and so,
The mind inherits
        the burden
        of

Grotesque
Absurdities
Del pasado.

Thus,
A
Mind is not,
Alas, a sealed-forever-heart!

La mente, al contrario,
Is an omniscient,
Indigenous,
Unyielding thing
That
    Knows!

And remembers!

Where does it find
Compassion to forget long
Enough to
    FORGIVE?

JOSÉ MONTOYA

Homage to Chagall

Your face
half blue
tortured palms
on winter canvas
paint a cock's head
above a broken doll
an unseen ghost
spits fire
under the tick
of the half-moon
a street-lamp walks
you kiss an angel's
head growing on red
wings burn
your cheek
a green beast
pulls a sleigh
over the white city
your family?
and you
alone in the street
your long hair
curled by the night
talk with angels
while sparks fly
from your brushes
and keep you warm
your palette breaks
the beating wind.

KATHLEEN TEAGUE

The Golden-Eyed Crossbow

for P. Lamantia

1 Under the sky's
   armpit
   a vision as hard
   as a pearl

2 The water's opaline
   eyes
   on the red runway

3 The fan
   was called Cyclone
   like the hatchet of the wind

4 Islands & mountains
   flowers
   & kiddies' rings

5 Blue prairies
   like the bronze of eyes
   & arrows of fire

CLAUDE PÉLIEU

Carmel Valley, 1968

The Moon

The night we went up into the rising hills and climbed up into the Moon who make me fiery lear
      & greener out of my eyes
She shone very bright;
And up the slopes where the deer skittered away up into the trees' antlers alone
Crooked against the Moon where they stood brandishing the black branches of the tribe male lover
      rearing in the sheets of the holy Moon
I gleaming raised my eyes
Powerfully, and the light clattered & hissed, to show my seeing to be strong and good.

Then, from far away in the country of the old
The snakes that are coiled in the rocks of the hills are whispering
To women driven mad as snakes in the baptismal silver of the Moon;
Yea & up to the Moon went the cries of the women, torn from their hair
And down shone the centuries that lie between us tonight;
And listening thus and thus receiving, we the two of us skipped down the moonlit hillside with our two
      shadows before us skipping down
Hearing the rich men's dogs, barking at the moonshine
Barbed wire in their teeth against the anarchy of light
From the rich men's hills beyond the lake
Old, gambling bones for their musty stakes.

Ah, Honey, the others have deserted me, I know you will never desert me, I said, and again I say she is mine
Round & full, she sets me talking out of my head like hands rattling in silver,
Sprinkling down like rain, and to that song
Come the jet-black and green-eyed women haunting
With the barbed silver and the two-edged flashing sword in the Moon of walking forever with her
Never beside me always beyond me Mary in the Moonlight wailing in the faraway hills, down to the jet
      jet black shore, to the river, down to the liquid light.

And down this mountain hillside I cannot fail to see, in the talking light
Some old dead Irishman, shining of the Moon.

CHARLES UPTON

Salute!

To every animal who eats or shoots his own kind
And every hunter with rifles mounted in pickup trucks
And every private marksman or minuteman with telescopic sight
And every smalltime con or bigtime gangster with gat
And every armed guard and every armed robber
And every redneck in boots with dogs and sawed-off shotguns
And every peace officer with dogs trained to track and kill
And every blackbelt master of any police karate academy teaching painless death
And every plainclothesman or private-eye and under-cover agent with shoulder-holster full of death
And every servant of the people gunning down people or shooting-to-kill fleeing felons
And every Guardia Civile in any country guarding civilians with handcuffs and carbines
And every border guard at no matter what Check Point Charley
    on no matter which side of which border Berlin Wall Bamboo or Tortilla Curtain
And every elite state trooper highway patrolman in custom-tailored riding pants and plastic crash-helmet
    and shoestring necktie and six-shooter in silver-studded holster
And every prowl-car with riot-guns and sirens and every riot-tank with mace and tear-gas.
And every crack pilot with rockets and napalm under wing and every sky-pilot blessing bombers at take-off
And any State Department of any super-state selling guns to both sides
And every revolutionary on any side whose gun comes first & last in the redemption of mankind
And every nationalist of no matter what nation in no matter what world Black Brown or White
    who kills for his nation
And every prophet or poet with gun or shiv and any enforcer of spiritual enlightenment with force
    and any enforcer of the power of any state with Power
And to any and all who kill & kill & kill for Peace
I raise my middle finger
In the only proper salute

LAWRENCE FERLINGHETTI

Santa Rita Prison, January, 1968

Come

Come let us journey to
      the Sky,
I promised the Moon.

All that I come from
All that I have been,
All that I am
All that I come to
All that I touch,
Blossoms from
      a thorn,
AROSEAROSE

Love is the condition
of Human Beings
Being Humans.

To be beloved
Is all I need
And whom I love
Is loved indeed,
There never was a Night that
Ended, or began,

Forms breaking
Structures imaged,
Come love,
Love come.

BOB KAUFMAN

Trying to Forget

In Hollywood, the air was quiet
in Beverly Glen above Sunset
Boulevard, the night fog clouded
by the stars, and August leaves brushed

after dinner, mist from oncoming day.
Difficult to remember one week stay
in a town loaded with memories
of another era, another frieze.

Where was I as Greta Garbo? Where had my
house gone, my clothes, my books surely
I could find a studio somewhere, but, no,
only a good friend provided hollow

shelter against a curious traveller, Pauline Rothschild.
Buried in name and a career, created, styled
as Rudolph Valentino, David O. Selznick and Jean Harlow.
How broke the shell without a dime, Norma Jean Monroe?

We travelled to friends, swimming pools
just one on Pacific Palisades, a
gracious memory of Miss England, her mother
prepared all afternoon the most difficult repast, while

the boys played billiards, and we danced, Shirley
Morand spoke of Henry Miller against her
husband's wishes, the luxury of California
the mystery of sparkling lights above Los Angeles,

the tanned limbs of Joan Collins, the profile of John Barrymore, Jr.
at the bar, Hampton Fancher, the III, and Dean
Stockwell accepted my "invitation" to follow us
to Tucson, after antiques for his Eugene O'Neill home.

JOHN WIENERS

May Mobilization

White sunshine on sweating skulls
Washington's monument pyramided high cloud granite
Over a soul mass, children screaming in their brains on quiet grass
(Black man strapped hanging in blue denims from an earth cross) —
Soul brightness under blue sky
Assembled before White House filled with mustached Germans
& police buttons, army telephones, CIA Buzzers, FBI bugs
Secret Service walkie-talkies, Intercom squawkers to Narco Fuzz & Florida Mafia Real Estate Speculators.
One hundred thousand bodies naked before an Iron Robot
Nixon's brain Presidential cranium case spying thru binoculars
From the Paranoia Smog Factory's East Wing.

ALLEN GINSBERG

May 9, 1970

Madimba: Gwendolyn Brooks

"Music is its own heartbeat"

Double-conscious sister in the veil,
Double-conscious sister in the veil;
Double-conscious sister in the veil:
Double-conscious sister in the veil.

You beat out the pulse with your mallets,
the brown wishbone anemones
unflowered and unworn in Chicago congo
prints, images, otherness, images

from the fossilbank: Madimba.
Black man; I'm a black man; black —
A-um-ni-pad-me-hum —
another brother gone:

"the first act of liberation
is to destroy one's cage" —
a love supreme;
a love supreme.

Images: words: language
typing the round forms: Juneteenth,
baby, we free, free at last:
black man, I'm a black man.

A garden is a manmade vision,
rectangular, weeded, shelled,
pathed, hosed, packed in,
covered with manure, pruned;

I own you; you're mine, you
mine, baby: to bear unborn things.
Double-conscious sister in the veil:
Double-conscious sister in the veil.

Black woman: America is artful
outside time, ideal outside space;
you its only machine: Madimba:
Double-conscious sister in the veil.

MICHAEL S. HARPER

Note: "double-consciousness" and
the "veil" refer to W.E.B. DuBois'
insights into white supremacy in the
seminal The Souls of Black Folk;
"Madimba" is an African instrument
of music without any metal parts.

Sunday, Guadalajara

August afternoon.
Silence.   Sleep.   The city
Has a terminal disease,
Is breathing quietly
And dying.   Ten
Miles away
At Zapopan,
The Church in heat.
The sweatless Virgin stands,
A plaster saint.
She clutches her Miraculous Son
To a bosom painted white.
All the standing Saints are mute.
Before them in the gloom
Candles burn all day, all night,
Are burning now.
Outside, the great
Aztec sun
Bakes the worn
Plaza, scrub
Trees, and
From here to there
Flat miles of clay.

ANTHONY OSTROFF

second Sapphic fragment / fainetai moi

phantom to me
that man like some god who
sits close to
and hears you

the laugh that
turns him on terrifies
me makes
my heart jump
speech stop

when I look at you
my tongue goes numb
& a fire runs thru
my veins
my eyes
don't see
ears roar

I become wet
and tremors
seize me

seeing you
& having no money
is like dying

Sappho
Translated by HARVEY BIALY

Confrontation

The mantis with translucent grin
climbs up the wrack of his six awkward limbs.

So on my palm he settles,
vein to colder vein,
stares from a steep face, bony as a stallion's
at my enormous focus:

the simple and the chambered eye.

JOHN HART

The Discovery of the Pacific

They lean against the cooling car, backs pressed
Upon the dusts of a brown continent,
And watch the sun, now Westward of their West,
Fall to the ocean. Where it led they went.

Kansas to California. Day by day
They travelled emptier of the things they knew.
They improvised new habits on the way,
But lost the occasions, and then lost them too.

One night, no-one and nowhere, she had woken
To resin-smell and to the firs' slight sound,
And through their sleeping bag had felt the broken
Tight-knotted surfaces of the naked ground.

Only his lean quiet body cupping hers
Kept her from it, the extreme chill. By degrees
She fell asleep. Around them in the firs
The wind probed, tiding through forked estuaries.

And now their skin is caked with road, the grime
Merely reflecting sunlight as it fails.
They leave their clothes among the rocks they climb,
Blunt leaves of iceplant nuzzle at their soles.

Now they stand chin-deep in the sway of ocean,
Firm West, two stringy bodies face to face,
And come, together, in the water's motion,
The full caught pause of their embrace.

THOM GUNN

104

To R—*Before Leaving to Fight in Unknown Terrain* / Havana, 1969

Mass media I adore you,
with a whisper in the microphone,
I touch the mass belly against mine,
like on a rush hour bus,
but with no sweat and no embarrassment.
"Don't die," I whispered, in person.
Only the air and revolutionary slogans hung between us.
"When I die I'll wear a big smile."
And with his finger painted a clown's smile
on his Indian face
"Don't die!" the whisper beneath the call to battle.
My love of man in conflict,
with my love for this man

Women die too.
They let go their tight grip on breath and sigh,
and sigh to die.
They say that Tania died before Che.
I saw her die in a Hollywood movie,
her blood floated in the river.
I stand in the street in Havana.
There are puddles here.
But few consumer goods to float in them.
Here the blood is stirred by the sacrifice of smiles
To armed struggle.
A phrase and an act.
They leave one day and they are dead.
"Death to the known order. Birth to the unknown."
Blood. Blood. Blood.
The warmth of it between the thighs
soothes the channel
out of which the baby fights and tears

I stand by a puddle in Havana
a woman full of blood,
net yet spilled.
Can I spill blood by my own volition?
Now it flows from me by a call of the moon,
The moon,
    a woman mopping her balcony
    spills water from her bucket
    on my hair, my breasts
    and into the puddle.
The question is answered.

NINA SERRANO

107

Sonsito

it is from the lips   from the lip blowing flying songy
it is from the maracas playing sheesheeshee to everything
to the base player who can hear whirling above his face

here they come bringing chocolate bringing heat
rubbing their shadows on the walking floor   out to the moony
light of secrets

'It is the wavy strength of ritmo'
you heard   you saw
son
son
sonsito

VICTOR HERNANDEZ CRUZ

The First Generation

Elegy to my grandmother

Bent and knotted as a wintered vine
she watched her daughters grow from her
in a hybrid land
and the grandchildren thick around
no longer her own.

Hototogisu naki naki
(The cuckoo cries cries

She grew wisteria
as a temple
in her garden
and there kept her private peace

Oto hitori ame de ato
the only sound after rain

The children mocked old ways
shook the fragile vines in their play
while silently she made a wreath
of the dying blossoms

shizuka no jimen arau
washes the land with quiet)

Her love wore long
as my sorrow.
The withered roots
have given back beauty to the soil.

JANICE MIRIKITANI

In Flight

He looks out the window

Thirty thousand feet of cumulus ascends
And grazing it his wingtip disappears

They turn, his window dips
Looking out he sees the ocean
Dallying below, parading shadows
Blow toward shore.

They level out on course, his window
Facing westward now, the coast slides by

The Cape is barely visible, the tall white surf
He gamboled yesterday and saw at takeoff
Now too small to see. Their island home
Behind the hills invisible. The base
No more than a vague white stripe
Across the dull green Cape Cod pines.

Cumulus towers stand along the course
Inside the clouds the airplane bumps
Gently, the windshield frosts, rain
Drives streaming against the glass
And disappears in sudden sunlight
On the other side. He counts the clouds
Looking out the window, forgets
How many clouds, the many hours
In flight away from her.

PATRICK SMITH

Serene Art

You, who
Are more like
A little girl
Than a woman
Who are older
Than me
But who most often
Seems younger
Engaged in various activities
I know nothing about
Watch in happy ignorance
As you move around the house

Sometimes, I see us asleep here
As from a distance, like two boulders
Propped in the shadows, by earth and stones

With marvelous ingenuity
You prepare my meals; I trust
The wheat . . . the meat and potatoes
You bring me

Now we sit at the windows and stare
At the light on the sea
And when the sun sinks into the water
And night falls
I go out
Hoist a log on my shoulders
And return with it
To the house
Where you are waiting

A woman falls from grace
Holy pictures
Join her

"The Battle Hymn
Of the Republic"
Is her favorite song
She stands in front of the mirror
All day long
Singing "T B H O T R"
All day long

With great pleasure
I remember the day I first saw her

Take off

LEWIS WARSH

Waiting in the Cafe

1. I wait in the cafe for my wife like a gorilla
   promoted to pull a red wagon
   with a blond in it
   through the Circus.
2. It's raining.
3. The rain thumps on the awning.
4. Paranoia takes the shape of a vulture
   washing down its dinner
   of tourists. The Gray Line Bus
   passes. They disboard. They run into the red lobby.
   Anne is late.
   My watch quacks in my pocket.
5. The vulture lifts its clean beak.
   Its neck a shining intestine.
6. I open my book of translations
   and flutter the pages
   and stop on
   these words: *moths,*
   crackling like sugar underfoot.
7. In the drugstore on the corner
   a sequence of flashbulbs goes off.
   Then a woman's laughter,
   like at an unbelievable threat to her body.
8. A maroon limousine stops at the light. The chauffeur
   wears a black cap and his passenger
   is the color of paper. An umbrella's
   hook at her cheek. From the waist up
   she is a lamp, a table lamp.
   It moves passed.
9. Anne is late again. Nearby,
   a yellow newspaper rack. I can read
   the headline. It says:
   TROOP CUTBACK HINTED. Above the fold

   there is a photograph of a blond in a swimming suit
   astride an enormous turtle.
   A newspaper left on the table behind me
   blows up. Giant paper heart
   attacks my chair.
10. Inside, the bartender polishes glasses.
    His cummerbund is on his shoulder.
    I flutter the pages to this:
11. *Green laurel lives on in the kitchen,*
    the voice doesn't change.
    What the fuck does that mean?
    I read it again, in context. "Dora Markus," 1939, Montale.
    It is a pretty picture. I get an insight:
    love of the grotesque begins with fear of the body.
12. Christ's blood. Picasso. Rimbaud. Enrapture.
    Anne, where are you?
13. The bartender is putting the chairs on the tables.

STAN RICE

(quotes from Robert Lowell's *Imitations*)

1

involuntary flex
fear
muscles bunched
around the eyes in my back

      slow jiggle of the haft as I walk
      pulls the blade
      the blade tears

some slight arrogance of
my pretty woman's body
the knife releases
the hand
has already disappeared

2

clumsy with
sunday
      the slow sun of
      his hands on male tools
drill
hammer
      the old rocking chair comes together
again
      as we do

JEANETTA JONES

up against the wall
he does not know

the surge
freedom from suffering

but expects it
unaware

of other
rooms   (space)
other walls

desire

clouds
his way,

a way
that becomes
his

and that passion
deprives him

the wall
not met

and therefore solid

without doors

what brings him to it
course of that desire?

does chaos, inactivity,
demand the possible?

eros known
springs other desires

other walls

DAVID GITIN

121

Figures and Ground

> Degas said he didn't paint
> what he saw but what
> would enable them to see
> the thing he had.
> — Jack Gilbert

a new diet:
there's less of me
I'm noticed more
my friends alarmed and call

so: it is what isn't
there
which gives value
to what is

in anything.
these lines

In His Poems Are El Greco's Hands

Wallace Stevens

Here. The silence echoes. Here.
The silence. At his ends no
end. Gibraltars to uneasy easy
Waters. His poetry also: uncaring
breaks. Onto my shores and sucking.
Me into. Vast void where the heart
he is a way to.

ROBERT LEVERANT

The Photo,

look at it!

a ship I thought
then,
and now: just a bathtub
with sails
and a lot of people:
Mother Father Erik Henning Sven
Uncle Oscar Vanja & Aunt Stina
all the friends & all their kids
Bertil Uffe Hasse Roffe Svante
Inga Lill & Britta
& Anmargret

everybody smiling
in the sun in the boat.

Tuck it back into the album
expand your sight
across its edges
let go
sail away
wave farewell

to them all
most friendly
to the unknown ones
But those I love;

the sadness
at the thought
my sails go slack
drift white
their shadows
flap
above me
cold

picture

now reversed
black teeth

smiling
in the negative.

LENNART BRUCE

Perspective

After Sylvia Plath

We sit, staring at books. Cut off from
The pages, there's our communal terror.
The children are down for the night.
Stubborn as sight, I want you to talk.
Let me flicker back on, swim towards
The stem of your face. It's raining

Outside. Even the heavens are less
Than empty. How shall I put us
Together again?

I'm inventing a monologue. One voice
For two. Or none will do. We'll sit
Here and let the town go mad.
They'll drown while I dream of
The Mediterranean
Of a white spanish house

Scalloped along a safe seacoast.

I'll be your fat mushroom of light,
Your salad, your silver, an icicle
Queen, to stagger and rattle the pots
And the pans. A face that stares back
Of the children's eyes, an orange pupil

Of the sun. And I'll be your opulent
Silent wife. All that you wanted. Success.

ADRIANNE MARCUS

Shaman Songs 12

We have made hawks
that fly
where no hawks have flown.

We have made hard sky
and look out at the rain.

We have made warm hides
From no animal yet slain.

We have made horses
that stride
as no horses ever known.

     But, we are weak.
     On our wounded plains, we are alone.

We have forgotten
the shape and cry of our bellies.

We have forgotten
the dances of our own faces,
the songs of our own voices.

We have forgotten
the chants of the souls
in our running feet.

     Now, we remember.
     In our weeping tents, we are alone.

GENE FOWLER

Yin and Yang

It is spring once more in the Coast Range
Warm, perfumed, under the Easter moon.
The flowers are back in their places.
The birds back in their usual trees.
The winter stars set in the ocean.
The summer stars rise from the mountains.
The air is filled with atoms of quicksilver.
Resurrection envelops the earth.
Geometrical, blazing, deathless,
Animals and men march through heaven,
Pacing their secret ceremony.
The Lion gives the moon to the Virgin.
She stands at the crossroads of heaven,
Holding the full moon in her right hand,
A glittering wheat ear in her left.
The climax of the rite of rebirth
Has ascended from the underworld
Is proclaimed in light from the zenith.
In the underworld the sun swims
Between the fish called Yes and No.

KENNETH REXROTH

                         Still
                                          our breath our sun
                           our moon, our stars, our space
                          our water that flows
                     out of the mountain, our ocean, our roads, our paths
                                     and into this year and into the next
                                 into the warm grey day, the damp smells rising
                           up out of the earth.
                                                     See, we can learn to move gracefully
                                          through this past learning
                                    this is a dream about 2 sources
                                                of image and language
                                                    about strength and ease
                                green tips that are fingers
                         pointing to the sky
                                                in the sun in the mist
                                    on the hill across
                                                        I remember spring now in summer
                                          in sun petals
                                        the quick grass springs back a vehicle
                                 for what passes through
              not for identity of I's and sorrows
                          struck by the humility total of truth
                     listening to separate existence of worlds
                            since I was born
                                      to look at substance
                            of what passes by the eyes
                                                      sparkling
                               in pages of notes of music
                             and remain in memory as renewal
                           as voices from out on the water
                               as craft
                         that carries those voyagers forward, back
                           out of time, is this moment
                              when I write to you
                                 these notes of myself

                                                    JOANNE KYGER

132

Filtres

One transluscent magenta leaf on a hot house plant is illumined through the window by cold morning light. Beyond that glass, winter blossoms of the same color, opaqued pink by the addition of white, adorn a small tree. This home is warm. I would as leave stay as go for the day invites me out-of-doors and by night I am welcome back again. Tomorrow I see her step through stream into the bath, and squat ever so gracefully before the altar of her toilet, hair long down her back, skin clear as her mind. Clouds shall issue from my mouth when I leave this house today. Love will billow, loves do bloom; may our love last like an empty purple bottle, survivor of several desert summers, gradually changing color under seasonal suns.

ANDREW HOYEM

From *Of Being Numerous*

It is difficult now to speak of poetry —

about those who have recognized the range of choice or those
who have lived within the life they were born to —. It is not
precisely a question of profundity but a different order of
experience. One would have to tell what happens in a life,
what choices present themselves, what the world is for us,
what happens in time, what thought is in the course of a life
and therefore what art is, and the isolation of the actual

I would want to talk of rooms and of what they look out on
and of basements, the rough walls bearing the marks of the
forms, the old marks of wood in the concrete, such solitude
as we know —

and the swept floors. Someone, a workman bearing about
him, feeling about him that peculiar word like a dishonored
fatherhood has swept this solitary floor, this profoundly hid-
den floor — such solitude as we know.

One must not come to feel that he has a thousand threads
     in his hands,
He must somehow see the one thing;
This is the level of art
There are other levels
But there is no other level of art

GEORGE OPPEN

From *The New Antigone*

CHORUS

Twenty five years of the endless war.

Earth and sea rise against us. Fish not fit to eat.
No bird-song. Plastic fruit and flowers.
The wine turns vinegar in the priest's chalice.

Twenty five years of the endless war.

Grain is blasted by mercury. Oil murders the birds.
I see a vast field of rubbery plants
Coated with poisonous dust, not a mammal, not a bird,
Not an insect. It stretches for thousands of miles.

We can destroy ourselves many times over. We have
Raped the moon and found it barren. Pity
Is no longer possible. The sorrow is too great.

Twenty five years of the endless war.

Rats flourish in the cities. Alligators in the sewers.
We might find fossil microbes on Mars or Venus.
The bodies float down the Mekong.
                              The east is red
With blood and exploding missiles. The Mekong Delta
Is fertile with the compost of corpses.
Antigone has given up weeping. The sorrow is too great.

Twenty five years of the endless war.

SECOND CHORUS

Antigone, we will go with you
To the shades of the final prison.
We will rise with you to our immolation.
We will fall with you
Toward Immortal Justice.
If we forget you, O Antigone,
May our cities crumble,
If your name is lost to our children
May they know no joy.

THOMAS PARKINSON

The Starface

Saved. Yet not saved.
You, like a star seen once
Float off to your distance,
Mornings & nights of distance,
Riding between us a fog bank
Thru which nothing is seen
Ever, ever. Stargone
Star to be foregone?
Nothing rising near
Hands, breast. Nothing
Shining my eyes since your face
Trailed to another sky cover,
Leaving me in the nolight of
Your going. Leaving me
The wound of your goneness.

MADELINE GLEASON.

Memoir

A hawk
      (I am a hawk)
A bittern

wings set far to the rear
      head and breast
thrust forward

soars above
      the Freeway
In the picture

you had just put up
      an osprey
untangled branches

looking for
      an unknown foe
The bittern

changed in flight
      wings curled
into horns

and the moon drove
      a Ram before
it in and out of focus

      I thought of
Jack   with a notebook
      and a glass of brandy
Robin spoke

of what moved
      an image   not an ideal
in   talk of Jack
      there was Jack

in the wire of words
      birds clutching bottles
I among them

and whoever went looking for
Jack found longing
I went to the bar awhile back, found

      birds caught in
swinging doors
      When Jack died

I thought of a genie in a bottle
that there would be no carcass

for the wealth had gone
I had seen a part of it

Whoever went longing
found what he looked for,

a fluttering in the bar —
a pale light ringing the table.

As I came here,
      invited to late dinner,
Jack's fable

      fell into place.
This food
      is blessed

casually
      the image breaks
Robin spoke   You   answered

what constant-
      ly seemed
impelled outward.

DAVID SCHAFF

143

Only the Sky

there is only the sky
barking at the passing moon
— *Franklin Rosemont*

Your head is so fragrant tonight that only the sky is above it
The sky like its own dog star desiring its luminous neighbor
I have listened patiently to your emptiness
The void slightly out of focus praising my mistakes
I unroll my new cosmology where stars are identified by their smell
    and the nicknames of the moon make children laugh in school
Your emptiness is a slit in the night
The white stranger rolls like an intelligent ball through your past
In the garden of crew cuts without any heads
Suddenly I am positive the hundred story pyramid is full of your hair

PETE WINSLOW

After the Engraving

(for Tom Clark)

What I am fashioning
with my light chisel
is an amulet to hang
round my love's neck

against disaster
dwelling in the hollows
well below, a spell
to keep the evil there

where she will never let me go
to fetch one home, to petrify
& carve upon, so I am making-do
by cutting up some earlier craftsman's

amulet, & yet
it sets her loveliness off wonderfully
now it is done, & seems to
keep its charge, despite

the old man's admonition —
the old fool, for these meadows
to speak plainly, these haphazard
city streets, admit

of no surprise
to violate her pose
under our cool skies
woven of rocks soil & stones.

DAVID BROMIGE

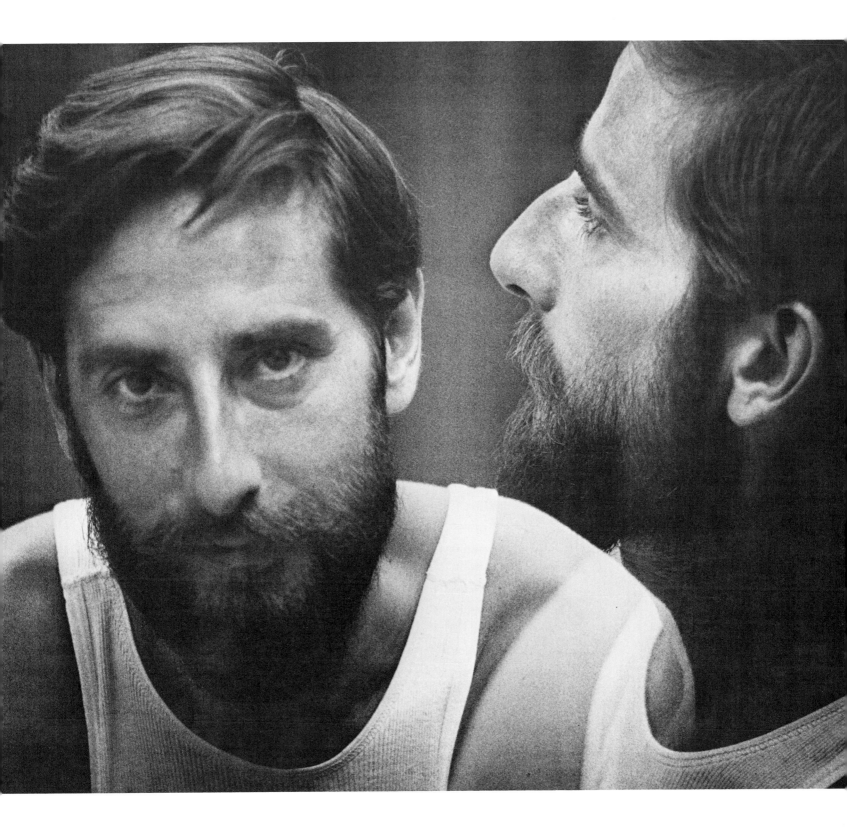

Attis

(for Harold Dull)

This is dying, to cut off a part of yourself
and let it grow

        The whole self
crawls at the thought of being mutilated,
even self-mutilated, as occurred to me
when you mentioned you had never looked at
the poem about Attis, and neither had I

nor at where in a poem feeling dries up —
A waterfall-filled Sierra canyon dammed
Hetch Hetchy of our spirit. Attis's
cock, in some tree, in some jug of wine
or beautiful lips mouthing Who we love
growing.

So the fireflies go, with small lunchboxes,
mooning around trees. We cut
our conversation off, too, in sacrifice

Birds,
brinks, even
our whole environment, out to the farthest star
you can never reach
(because of light's unchanging speed)
and so your dying can never reach either —

Blood,
not sinking into the ground, mysteriously,
but in the Roman sewers, forever, our home town.

GEORGE STANLEY

Song of Expectancy

I wait for her who restores my fingertips
I wait for the moons which will grow on my nails
I wait for the night with its intricate gloves
I wait for the skeleton keys

I wait for the emigrants in glass boats
For the rivers with their green hair
The synagogues which lie just under water
And the jewelled eyes in the willowtree

I wait for the ravens to settle on fencerails
With wings like Finnish wimples
I wait for the pinetrees to explode the stars
And for the clouds with their little windows of rain

I wait for the sheriffs who always arrive
With tomorrow manacled between them
I wait for the bandits and their crucified children
Who wear roses of gauze on their masks

For the ragmen who gather our hearts on spikes
The centurions pissing in cemeteries
The cowboys driving cadavers before them
And their yelping mutts whose fur is afire

I wait at last for ignorance and its subpoena
For silence with its headless drum and pews full
                              of empty hats
For sleep which pours in foam from the ribs
And for the dark sad waters where legends swim
                              backward like squid

GEORGE HITCHCOCK

Vanish

back to the roots
    of the grass
     white
      and black circles
   of earth, tiny tiny
       tiny
         mark the only
         limits of yr
    hands
      a dog barking
       an old lady
     playing the
         piano in a room full of
      grass that turned to light

JOHN OLIVER SIMON

Playing

1. *Eyes Closed*

My kid says   *I*
hope I die   soon
so I'll be an angel
and leans sidewise

Sun catches
me wide-eyed

Not as it slides
beneath the eyelids
of the peach
sunspots changing
to sugar

It's eaten
by a darkness
within me   the pit
waiting
at my core

2. *Eyes Open*

This morning's poem   hand
written on a long
sheet of rice paper   I rolled
like a spyglass
to look at this
child

giggly Colin
three year old   leans sidewise
to look back

How a poem may join
us   eye
and   eye
with   joy

PHILIP DOW

155

Realities

for George Oppen

When I've been warm
a long time, I don't think of any
fever in the absence of wind,
hum of a few bees, orange cat
dozing in the sun.

        The idea
I have of myself is the thing
that's corrupted. To move
from that,
        turning down sheets
at night, the skin
shines on the knuckles, fingers
pull at the fabric. Arm's swing,
shift of the elbow, stretch
at the wrist. Alive. My self
and nobody's mother.

The rest is comment.

        Or
one could say: stars,
grass the mountain—
letting them be.

But we continue,
"Yes, I see," meaning
not what the eye takes in
but what we know along with it

or maybe after
when we look again.

The way I hold this prism
to the sun

turning it sideways
to refract the light

until I see the rainbow
not the glass
the seven colors passing
through my hand.

SHIRLEY KAUFMAN

156

The Black Spring Becomes Anonymous

The wind is blowing in the scent of formaldehyde
for the barefoot and the blind
I approach my shadow like a two-gun gunman
of the Old West
You get the publicity and your father gets grey hairs.
Out of my breath comes the smell of formaldehyde
                on the Rose of Sharon
and the Rose of Sharon dies.

SOTÈRE TORREGIAN

The Number One Daughter of the Wang Family

Once we rode
      bamboo
      stick horses
            between your house and mine
Still I remember
       curly pigtails
       covering your neck
rouge
    dabbed on your forehead
Your mother
led you by the hand
         Your father
         carried you piggyback
Sometimes
      you put on boy's clothes
Though you were very small
         my heart
         hurt for you
After school
     when you got home before dark
you'd come up to my red room
        asking:
          Is the wild quince in bloom?
          Have you seen a goldfinch yet?
and beg me
    for a brush pen
    to paint your eyebrows
Twenty years
     over the world
        a long-time wanderer
and everything that's happened
       like a flaw of wind
       passing dream
mere rain and cloud
     dividing us

Today
     meeting again
         in this room
we still keep —
       shall I say? —
           certain affections
together with some evidence of sociability
Dear lady!
      do you remember
          years ago
         when you were shy and small
it needed
      only a word from me
          to get you all worked up
and your cheeks
      would turn
      bright pink?
I'd give
my right eye
     to see
       just that again!

Chen Hsieh

translated by
C. H. KWOCK

Waking at Night

Waking at night,
silver-wet
as a snake
shook from his old skin,
I know my quilt is the meadow
and that turning
I'll drag the whole field with me
into sleep.
I lie still
feeling the cold
trace the edges of my teeth,
moonlight
frosting the near sides of weeds;
and I'm standing
in the high place under the oak tree,
moonlight in the field below.
Small bones snap
as though something were breaking
in a far place
inside me:
shocks,
crackings,
words so small-boned
they collapse
before I can hear them.
Limps, smashed leaves,
trottings, scurryings
through tunnels of briar,
and the snout-nudgings
underground,
claw-whisks, splashes of dirt.
My boots bump against stones

in a running
I hadn't known
I'd begun —
the wind-whiskers
sleeked to my face,
the howling
in my ears,
as the whole field tips,
rises higher than trees
with beetle-sparklings,
flashes of eye, moon shell,
lightninged branches, milky leaves:
blocking the moonlight, the stars —
a rearing I run toward
which will collapse
into my map of bones.

MORTON MARCUS

The Diamond

Furl back black walls with shook Fire!
Curl back that skin of your hair.
Pull back eyelids covering water
pouring from the ONE SIGHT gazing over the Abyss!
Iron obsesses the stars! Swivelling in AUM grease
in iron galaxies, metal rods &
      aquarius pistons pump across eons of space
light-years jerting from the light-socket

Ink blots open out landscapes cut in half above solar orchards
golden hay piles, swirls of gold straw
        flusking across the wind.
Giant girls smile near the hay-wagon
      lounging on an axle, buxom.
Inner-cheek flesh promises sweets to the tongue flash
    in the sensual paradise miles away from
        the Detonation Center of NoPlace.
The blast shakes windows but the doors of Hell firm in their hinges
    hot to the touch!
    And the tunnel Unexposed except to the
      Diamond-Cutter.

Furl back black anthracite coal-shafts to the
    pure unsullied Diamond sallying forth
      out of hiding
parting and cleaving its subtle facets in
clear cut incisive flasks faceting
the waters of the Eye shining diamond brightness
watching miles undersea.
So that not the Names, the Divine Names of Known Gods
but the shadow sliced open against sunlight

    clear-cut, straight to walk out on!

DANIEL MOORE

With the sun —
fear leaves me
rushes to cover/
leaves lumps
like the backyard gopher
to remind me

I am afraid
of anyone
of anything
that would harm me/
not the pain
not the act
but,
    the desire.

PATRICIA PARKER

The Passport

On the back porch
of his mother's house, a clown
watches the wind
making grass into flags.

He thinks a trip to the doctor
will bring back
his dream of the ocean.

Somewhere he saw a sign that read
'A medicine ball will be given
to all those in favor
of playing the game.'

The batteries begin and end
in the palm of his hand —
one zone gives way to another.

Drunken bottles are screaming,
the underwear seem to be chipmunks,
a girl unbuttons her blouse,
love shrugs its shoulders;

a child discovers the teeth
that have power over the shadows,
spiders are singing
to someone the trees have forgotten

and the streams are flooding the meadows
with the blood
of pearls.

LUIS GARCIA

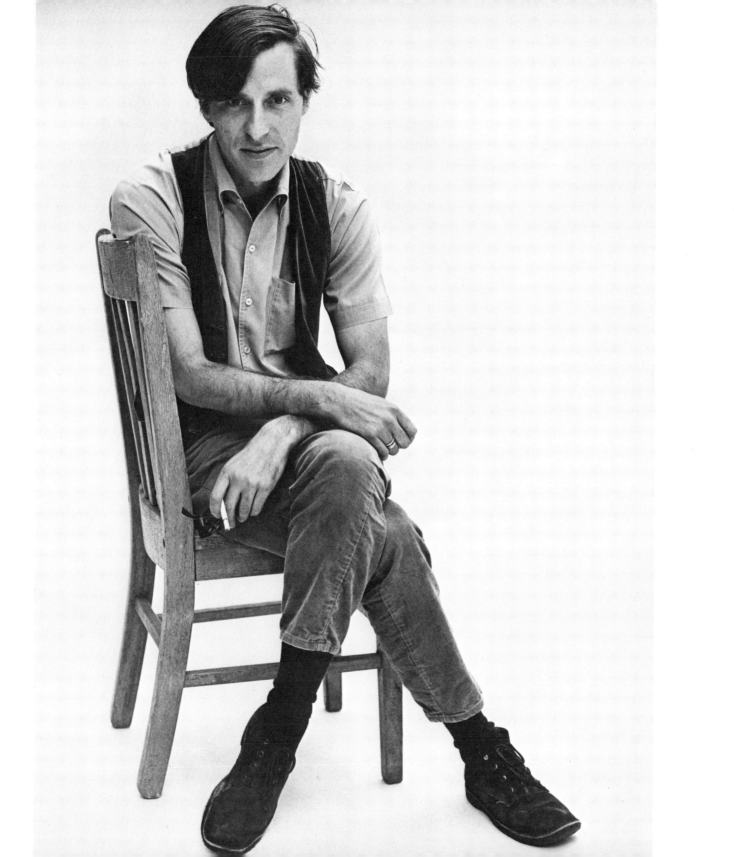

On Pure Sudden Days like Innocence

On pure sudden days like innocence
we behold the saints and their priorities
    keypunched in the air.

Curiously Young like a Freshly=Dug Grave

Curiously young like a freshly-dug grave
the day parades in circles like a top
    with rain falling in its shadow.

RICHARD BRAUTIGAN

Autobiographical Notes

The number in parentheses refers to the page on which the poet's work appears.

WILDER BENTLEY (25): Born in 1900, San Francisco; studied at Yale University and at the University of Michigan. After World War I he did relief work with French war orphans in the devastated area between Soissons and Chateau Thierry (1921) and later (1923–1926) spent three years in travel and study in Europe. At the present time he is teaching in the Humanities, Languages, and Literature division at San Francisco State College. His poetry has been published in *The Hudson Review* and elsewhere. His paintings and brush drawings have been exhibited in San Francisco, Los Angeles, and Detroit; he has had one-man shows in private galleries in New York City and in Madison, Wisconsin, as well as Florence, Italy.

JEFF BERNER (58): Born 1940, New York; founded *Stolen Paper Review* (1962); various happenings and exhibitions in Prague, San Francisco, and Stanford, California. Published in various periodicals and anthologies, including *Antioch Review*, *Robho* (Paris), *Once Again* (N.Y.), and *Kayak* (S.F. and Santa Cruz). Forthcoming: *The Innerspace Project* (World Publishing Co., N.Y.) and *The Daily Planet* (Jonathan Cape Ltd., London, & Grossman, N.Y.). Resides in Mill Valley, California, with wife Penelope and circus-dog Rasputin.

HARVEY BIALY (100): Born NYC, 1945, (sun 2° Gemini, moon 28° Libra, Scorpio rising, neptune at midheaven). *Pierre Vidal in the garage of Arthur Avalon,* with rock & roll, *My Boyfriend's Back* blasting. The people are Timotha (=she-who-honors-the-goddess), Robert Kelly and Kenneth Anger; there is also a silverish dog walking around somewhere. (An ambiguity re. the moon, who doesn't I think like poems or poetry, although is a constant lover of poets) I see my poems as being created around my life, using poetry as a way of making it have meaning, all the worlds I move in. Essentially a process of discovery. It goes on, almost like writing on water.

Poems have appeared in *Caterpillar, Io, El Corno Emplumado, Matter, Chicago Review,* etc. Contributing editor of *Io.* Lecturer in Contemporary American Poetry at Mills College, 1967–68.

Books: *Love's Will* (Matter Press, 1968); *The Geronimo Poem* (Pothanger Press, 1969); *Susanna Martin* (Maya Quarto #7, 1970); *Babalon 156* (Sand Dollar Press, 1970).

KAY BOYLE (72) has published four volumes of poetry, seven collections of short stories, a collection of short novels, and three books for children. She has done numerous translations from the French, and served as foreign correspondent in France and Germany for *The New Yorker Magazine* for seven years. She is the author of thirteen novels, the most recent being *Generation Without Farewell* (Knopf, 1960).

Literary awards: Guggenheim Fellowships, 1934 and 1961; O. Henry Memorial Prize for the best short story of the year, 1934 and 1941. She has been a member of the English Department of San Francisco State College since 1963, and is at present completing a history of Germany for the Doubleday Mainstream of European History series.

RICHARD BRAUTIGAN (171) was born January 30, 1935, in the Pacific Northwest. He has lived in San Francisco for many years. He is the author of *Trout Fishing in America* (novel); *A Confederate General from Big Sur* (novel); *In Watermelon Sugar* (novel); *The Pill Versus the Springhill*

173

Mine Disaster (poetry); *Please Plant This Book* (poetry); *All Watched Over by Machines of Loving Grace* (poetry); *Rommel Drives On Deep into Egypt* (poetry); and *The Abortion: An Historical Romance of 1966* (novel) and *Revenge of the Lawn* (short stories), both due in 1971.

DAVID BROMIGE (146): It's hard to be certain, of what can be said, here, to define who I am. To my joy it's recently become possible to me, in part through my own efforts, to dwell on the side of this hill, southwest of Sebastopol, & thus removed from the habits that in Berkeley for seven years gave such definition to my life, I wonder. It seems that the country was always what drew me — 'David Bromige left London to work on farms in Sweden, the north of England, & Saskatchewan.' But my companion wears country dresses she bought on Telegraph Ave. — one sees their like all over — & very winsome she appears in them, here in 1970....

No matter Heracleitus thought the self began to disguise itself as soon as it approached self-revelation, you would be known. And will — but, will that be you. There are strands of circumstance, surely. That we can grasp, if we will, & the thread we are is felt by that. But the other strands in these threads? So, who I might be said to be, in this autobiographical note, eludes me. That rubric is what has to be reified, in present imaginations. The stories we tell ourselves by shall reckon with this fact, or come to nothing.

JAMES BROUGHTON (60): I am a third generation Californian. Most of my life has been lived in or near San Francisco, where my first books, films and plays were produced. But I have worked as journalist in New York, I have made a film in London, I have published a book in Paris, and I have made pilgrimages to Compostella, Jerusalem, and Angkor Wat. At present I live at the foot of Mt. Tamalpais with my wife Suzanna and my children, Serena and Orion, and I am employed at the San Francisco Art Institute and San Francisco State College.

My mother wanted me to become a surgeon. But when I was 3 years old I was wakened in the night by a glittering stranger who told me I was a poet and not to fear being alone or being laughed at. That was my first meeting with my angel, who is the best poet I have ever met.

When I was 10 I was sent to military school, where (thanks to my angel) I fell in love with the English language. I obtained unwillingly a bachelor degree from Stanford University. From there I went into the merchant marine, the New York Herald-Tribune, the off-Broadway theater, the New School for Social Research, experimental filmmaking, fine book printing, analytical psychology, Eastern philosophy, and teaching (in more or less that order.)

I have published 10 volumes of poetry, and my collected poems entitled *A Long Undressing* are scheduled for publication by the Jargon Society in Winter 1971. I have made one recording, *The Bard & the Harper,* reading my poems to the music of Joel Andrews. I have independently produced 8 films, the most recent being *The Bed* and *The Golden Positions.* I have a Guggenheim Fellowship for 1970–71.

LENNART BRUCE (124): I started writing 5 years ago after having lived in Europe, South America & West Africa active as a free lance mainly in food distribution, transport & housing. After the termination of my business activities I settled in San Francisco. I have published three books of poetry: *Making the Rounds* and *Observations* by Kayak Press and *Moments of Doubt,* Cloud Marauder Press, San Francisco. My fourth book, *The Mullioned Window* (Kayak Press), will be out shortly, and my fifth collection of poems, *Happy Landing,* will be printed in 1971. I have also published translations from the Swedish & Spanish languages.

VICTOR HERNANDEZ CRUZ (108) was born in Aguas Buenas, Puerto

Rico, 1949, and has lived in the United States since 1953. His work published in the following magazines: *Umbra, Negro Digest (Black World), Evergreen Review, Ramparts, For Now,* and *Journal of Black Poetry. Snaps* is his first book of poetry; it was published by Random House in 1969. He is currently living in Berkeley and working on a novel.

ALAN DIENSTAG (29) was born 3000 years ago on the island of Crete.

PHILIP DOW (155): Starting from Santa Fe (thirty-three years gone) I hunted the vanishing California wilderness from Vallejo, which I now like to think named for César. The next life began with Juanita and our sons, Dylan (today he asked "Can you stand on the rings around Saturn?"), and Colin.

At present in Buffalo, I miss San Francisco bread, the white sky, pheasant hunting with Mark Linenthal, my friends the prolific snails, and that occasional afternoon Dubonnet with Kay Boyle. Yet, here these stubby pudge-winged sparrows so bundled for fall they barely fly, and here Juanita and I lay listening to neverending thunder.

WILLIAM EVERSON (38): "Brother Antoninus"; left the Dominican Order in 1969 and now lives and works in Stinson Beach, California.

LAWRENCE FERLINGHETTI (88), probably born 1919 or 20 in Yonkers, New York. Some tampering with the birth certificate has been uncovered, some of it by himself. His mother was Clemence Monsanto, and he was her fifth and last son. She was enclosed in an asylum shortly after his birth which was itself preceded by the sudden death of his father. His father was an Italian auctioneer in Brooklyn who must have arrived WOP (With Out Papers) from Lombardy about the turn of the century. The family name was shortened to Ferling but restored by LF when of age. There was a French "aunt" who took LF to France in swaddling clothes where they remained for an uncertain number of years. Her name was Emily Monsanto, descended from that same Sephardic-Portuguese Mendes-Monsanto who emigrated to the Virgin Islands in a Danish Crown Colony expedition after the Spanish Inquisition and was there knighted by the King of Denmark. LF's first memory of America is eating tapioca pudding (undercooked, and called Cat's Eyes by the inmates) in an orphanage in Chapaqua, New York. He then spent many years in a mansion of a branch of the Lawrence family which founded Sarah Lawrence College in Bronxville, N.Y., where much-beloved Emily left him after serving as a French governess in that family. She later died in an asylum at Central Islip, Long Is-

land, unknown to LF. . . . As a poet, Ferlinghetti describes himself as an Unblinking Eye. He is now engaged in a long prose Work-in-Progress, one part of which is tentatively called, "Her Too." Books: *Pictures of the Gone World* (City Lights, 1955); *A Coney Island of the Mind* (New Directions, 1958); (trans.) Jacques Prevert, *Paroles* (City Lights, 1958); Her (novel; New Directions, 1960); *Unfair Arguments with Existence* (plays; New Directions, 1964); *The Secret Meaning of Things* (New Directions, 1968); *Tyrannus Nix?* (New Directions, 1969); *Back Roads to Far Towns* (City Lights, 1970); *Mexican Night* (New Directions, 1970).

GENE FOWLER (129) has lived many lives. Born Oct. 5, 1931, he has spent his life trying to become the world. He has studied widely in almost every field yet has no formal education. His published works are *Field Studies* (dust), *Quarter Tones* (Grande Ronde Press), *Shaman Songs* (dust), and soon, *Fires* (Grove). These are all poems. Other books soon to be published include a book of short stories and a pamphlet on the Tarot. This summer he is Visiting Artist for Poetry at the University of Wisconsin. He has made one film and is working into making more — it would be easier to list what he *doesn't* do than what he does. (*Hilary Ayer Fowler*)

LUIS GARCIA (168): Born Berkeley, Jan. 10, 1939. Schooling there; spent some time in South America, 1963–4.

ALLEN GINSBERG (94): Grammar & High School Paterson, N.J., B.A. Columbia College 1948; associations with Jack Kerouac, Wm. S. Burroughs, Herbert H. Huncke & Neal Cassidy begun 1945 NYC and next decade after with Gregory Corso, Peter Orlovsky companion 1954 & poets Michael McClure, Philip Lamantia, Gary Snyder & Philip Whalen in San Francisco became known 1955 on as "Beat Generation" and/or "San Francisco Renaissance" literary phases; acquaintance with William Carlos Williams 1948 & study of his relative-footed American speech prosody led to *Empty Mirror* early poems with W.C.W. preface, as later Williams introduced *Howl*.

Illuminative audition of William Blake's voice simultaneous with Eternity-vision 1948 & underground bust-culture Apocalypse-realization conduced 8-month stay NY State Psychiatric Institute and later preoccupation with Gnostic-mystical poetics and politics.

Participated in college poetry readings & NY literary scene '58–'61 with Leroi Jones & Frank O'Hara; Vancouver '63 & Berkeley '65 Poetry Conventions with Olson, Duncan, Creeley, Snyder, Dorn & other poet friends; Albert Hall Poetry Incarnation, readings with Vosnosensky in London, and anti-Vietnam War early Flower Power marches in Berkeley 1965. Attended mantra-chanting at first Human Be-in S.F. 1967. Mantric poetics & passing acquaintance with poet-singers Ezra Pound, Bob Dylan, Ed Sanders, Paul McCartney & Mick Jagger led to music study for tunes to Wm. Blake's *Songs of Innocence and Experience;* this homage to visionary poet-guru William Blake, occasioned by visit West Coast to touch a satin bag of body-ashes the late much-loved Neal Cassidy, & composed one week on return from police-state shock in Chicago, was recorded summer 1969 Aetat 43. Pallbore funerals late Kerouac & Olson, last few winters spent outside cities learning music milking cows & goats.

Poetry: *Howl & Other Poems* (City Lights Books, S.F., 1956); *Kaddish & Other Poems* (City Lights, 1961); *Empty Mirror* (early poems; Totem/Corinth, N.Y., 1961); *Reality Sandwiches* (City Lights, 1963); *Ankor Wat* (Fulcrum Press, London, 1968); *Airplane Dreams* (from journals; Anansi/City Lights, 1968); *Planet News* (City Lights, 1968). Prose: *Yage Letters,* with Wm. S. Burroughs (City Lights, 1963); *Indian Journals* (Dave Haselwood/City Lights, 1970). Phonograph Records: *Howl & Other Poems* (Fantasy/Galaxy Records, Oakland, 1959); *Kaddish* (Atlantic, 1966); *Wm. Blake's Songs of Innocence & Experience Tuned by Allen Ginsburg* (MGM, 1970).

DAVID GITIN (121): Born in 1941 (Sagittarius). Degree in Philosophy from Buffalo. Graduate work in Pittsburgh (English). Co-founded Poets' Theatre in San Francisco. Edited *Bricoleur* magazine.

Poems published throughout U.S., Canada, England and W. Germany, including an anthology; readings on KPFA and other radio stations, on television, in coffeehouses and galleries, etc.

MADELINE GLEASON (141), poet, painter and playwright, has lived and worked for many years in San Francisco. In 1947 Miss Gleason founded the Poetry Center, which twice yearly presented the Poetry Festivals, the first of their kind in America. A poet whatever her medium, she finds a close relationship between poetry, painting and song. In collaboration with composer John Edmunds, she has translated German lieder and the Anna Magdalena Notebook of Bach.

Her poems are lively parables of common sense and common nonsense, written from an uncommon sense of the predicament that lies between. Spirited and spiritual, they capture the many images of man in a variety of vivid forms and a lucid music. The same spirit moves in Miss Gleason's paintings, though they are less explicit, for whether she works with brush or pencil she discovers to us her own (our own?) ambiguous, awesome world.

Publications: *The Artist's View*, Claire Mahl, ed. (1952); *Poems* (Grabhorn Press, 1944); *The Metaphysical Needle* (Centaur Press, 1949); *Two Folios* (Unicorn Press, 1967, 1968); *Concerto for Bell and Telephone* (Unicorn Press, 1967). Plays: *Why in the World* (1960); *Here Comes Everybody* (1967).

RAFAEL JESÚS GONZÁLEZ (43): For the careful reader, there is no more intimate data on the poet's life than his verse. Beyond that there can only be facts. That I was born in El Paso, Texas, is significant only in that it made me heir to two muses who speak different languages and do not always get along well with each other. Served in the Navy Hospital Corps spending two years attached to the Marine Corps. Received my education at the University of Texas at El Paso, the National University of Mexico, and the University of Oregon. Have taught world literature and creative writing at the University of Oregon, Western State College of Colorado, and Central Washington State College. At the present time I am Chairman of the Department of Mexican and Latin American Studies at Laney College in Oakland. I see my life as motivated by a constant service to the ideals of beauty, love, and truth, which is to say that in this particular period of history in the U.S. it is not a very easy life to lead.

THOM GUNN (104): Born in England 1929. First came to California in 1954 and has lived in San Francisco for the last ten years. Books published: *Fighting Terms* (1954), *The Sense of Movement* (1957), *My Sad Captains* (1961), *Touch* (1967), *Moly* (1971).

MICHAEL S. HARPER (97): Born Brooklyn, N.Y., 1938. B.A., M.A., Cal. State, L.A.; M.A., University of Iowa. Publications: *Dear John, Dear Coltrane* (University of Pittsburgh Press, 1970); *History Is Your Own Heartbeat* (University of Illinois Press, 1971).

JOHN HART (102): Born in 1948 in Berkeley. Parents: teacher/critic Lawrence Hart and poet Jeanne McGahey. Since I began writing early, I was able during high school and college to accumulate a modest amount of publication of poetry, translation and reviews.

I am also very much interested in the problems of adequate translation of poetry. From 1966 to 1970, I studied translation in the Comparative Literature Department at Princeton University, and at the University of Freiburg in Germany. I'm now taking advantage of an award from the Phelan Foundation to study full time in the Lawrence Hart seminars in advanced poetic techniques.

DAVID HENDERSON (44): Born in Harlem; lived in New Orleans, Acapulco, Greenwich Village; now resides in Berkeley, California. Taught at City College of New York, Ocean Hill-Brownsville Experimental School District, Brooklyn, N.Y., University of California at Berkeley. Widely published in anthologies and periodicals. Books: *Felix of the Silent Forest* (Poets Press, 1967); *De Mayor of Harlem* (E. P. Dutton, 1970).

JAN HERMAN (18):
29 B Guy Place
San Francisco   16. Juni 1970

Dear Mr. Herman,
Mr. Rolf Herman has drawn ouer attention to jou. We are very interested in jour prospects inform us about jour work and achievements.

Yours very truly
Förderungsgemeinschaft
N.
R E G I A

GEORGE HITCHCOCK (150): Publisher of Kayak Books; lives in Santa Cruz. Four volumes of poetry.

ANDREW HOYEM (135): Born 1935, Sioux Falls, South Dakota. Has lived in California since 10th year. Following B.A. from Pomona College and a hitch in the Navy, was associated with The Auerhahn Press during the poetry renaissance in San Francisco. Travelled Orient 1957–59, Europe 1961 & 68. Works as printer and typographical designer.

Magazine appearances: *Poetry, Evergreen Review, Cow, F. U.: a magazine of the arts, Work, Blue Grass, Intransit, The World, Now, Prospect, For Now, Cassiopeia, Ambit,* etc.

Books: *The Wake,* early poems (Auerhahn Press, San Francisco, 1963-o.p.); *The Music Room* (Dave Haselwood Books, S.F., 1965-o.p.); *Chimeras,* transformations of Nerval's sonnet sequence (Dave Haselwood Books, S. F., 1966); *The Pearl,* translated from Middle English with John F. Crawford (Grabhorn-Hoyem, S.F., 1967). A new collection: *Articles: poems 1960–67* (Cape Goliard Press, London, and Grossman Publishers, New York, 1969).

JEANETTA L. JONES (119): Born 28 September 1947, 10:19 p.m. of three points of the compass

South, nine months in the womb nine months out

North, twelve years a solemn country child West, suburban highschool,

Mills College (2 units short of B.A. in Language and Myth)

emerging a little farther west in San Francisco, where I persuade a dim lofty-ceilinged pre-earthquake Victorian flat to be my home and that of The New American Poetry Circuit, which I direct.

BOB KAUFMAN (91) was first published in Beatitude Magazine in San Francisco in the late 1950's. His broadsides, "The Abomunist Manifesto," "Second April," and "Does the Secret Mind Whisper" were separately published by City Lights and then included in his first book, *Solitudes Crowded with Loneliness,* published by New Directions in 1965. This book was translated and published in France in a big pocketbook edition and immediately achieved a notoriety rare among books of poetry by foreign poets, with features in leading French revues such as *l'Express, La Quinzaine, Jeune Afrique,* and *Jazz Magazine.* Today in France Kaufman is considered among the greatest Negro-American poets alive in spite of his continuing exclusion from American anthologies, both Hip & Academic. (*City Lights*)

SHIRLEY KAUFMAN (156) is the 1969 United States Award winner of the International Poetry Forum. Her winning manuscript, *The Floor Keeps Turning,* was published in 1970 by the University of Pittsburgh Press.

Born in Seattle, Washington, she studied drama at the University of Washington, received her B.A. from UCLA and her M.A. from San Francisco State College, where she won the Academy of American Poets' Prize in 1964.

Her poems have appeared in *The Atlantic, Choice, Harper's, Kayak, New American Review, The New Yorker, The Nation, The Quarterly Review of Literature, Poetry, Poetry Northwest, The Southern Review* and other journals. Her work has been included in three of the Borestone Mountain Poetry Award Annuals, the latest in *Best Poems of 1969,* and the Doubleday Anchor anthology, *Quickly Aging Here—Some Poets of the 1970's.*

Married and the mother of three daughters, Mrs. Kaufman, in collaboration with Nurit Orchan, has translated from the Hebrew the book-length poem *My Little Sister,* by the Israeli poet Abba Kovner. Penguin will publish this work in its Modern European Poets Series in 1971.

She is working now on a new collection of poems, and continuing her translations of a number of Israeli poets.

DAN KENNEY (26): Born in New York City uncomfortably close to fifty years ago. Experienced the usual educational disasters. Better forgotten. Attended college in N.Y. briefly, University of South Dakota, U.C. Berkeley without working toward a degree, taking courses I expected to enjoy. Best way to attend college is to use the facilities, especially the library, avoid boring courses and above all boring professors. If you don't cultivate a spirit of enthusiasm and exuberance in college you're dead.

Grew up mainly on Long Island during depression years, escaping for the most part the misfortunes of that era. Plenty of space for variety of activities: fields, woods, swamps, endless water resources; away from school great freedom from interference from adults. All extremely important in the lives of children. Housed, clothed, fed and loved by the adults important to me. Only possible basis of satisfactory relations between children and adults. Years from fourteen to eighteen were very bad bringing constant interference from small minded, self-serving, fatuous men and women. This was a period of personal spiritual upheaval and searching; school curricula and teachers absolutely irrelevant; made considerable progress in resolving conflicts in spite of them and without any help from them at all.

Worked at a variety of occupations, none worth mentioning. Never good at making money; for the most part couldn't care less. I loaf a lot; read; paint.

MARY NORBERT KÖRTE (21): Born, 1934, raised in California, the usual education: nursery through graduate school, with various attendant honors and degrees that seemed important at the time (I used to play the piano for fond parents and friends, too). Member of Dominican Order 1952–68, consequent and heavy religious influence; now on the long and cliche-ridden road to finding self.

C. H. KWOCK (160): Born Honolulu (1920), of Chinese parentage. Studied under private tutors until old enough (after twenty) to do extensive traveling and research at Harvard, University of Tokyo, University of Hong Kong, and the Academia Sinica in Taiwan. Newspaper editing in Honolulu, San Francisco and New York City. Retired from newspaper work in 1965 and since then has been working for the U.S. government. Books: *Why I Live on the Mountain* & *The Lady and the Hermit* (translations of Chinese poetry, with Vince McHugh), *Chinese Mother Goose, The Bull with Magic Eyes* & *The Tiger Rider* (vols. of Chinese fables and epigrams respectively), *Leaves in the Wind* (Japanese haiku and senryu), and *Hakka Folk Songs*.

JOANNE KYGER (132) has lived in many different places; born in Vallejo, California, she spent her early childhood in China, before returning to the states for short stays in Florida, Detroit, Hollywood, Honolulu & Santa Barbara. She's lived in India & Japan for long periods of time; in San Francisco & New York City. Her first book, *The Tapestry and The Web,* was published by The Four Seasons Foundation. Her poems have appeared in many magazines, among them: *Coyotes Journal, Wild Dog, Angel Hair, The Paris Review, Poetry, The World, Stony Brook, Caterpillar* and *Sugar Mountain.* A second book, *Places To Go,* was published by Black Sparrow in 1970. She presently lives in Bolinas, California.

DANIEL J. LANGTON (57) was born in Paterson, New Jersey; raised in East Harlem, Manhattan; and considers San Francisco his permanent home. His early writing was guided by William Carlos Williams, Richard Duerden and Robert Stock, to whom he remains consciously grateful. He wants to be stolid and important, and his poems thought of as rocks.

ROBERT LEVERANT (122): born boston july 5, 1939; influences: life, reading; teachers: jack wolfe, v.c. jog, jacquelyn, fritz perls; kirpal singh, guru. profession: photographer; author: *zen in the art of photography.* vegetarian.

AMÍLCAR LOBOS (69) received his M.A. at San Francisco State College. In 1968, he acted for Sevilla Films,

Madrid; in 1969 was part-time consultant for Casa Espana de Bellas Artes, Inc.; is now its Executive Director. He is a part-time consultant on Latin-American culture for the S.F. State College Teacher Corps and Community Liaison for the University of California and the Mission district of San Francisco.

ADRIANNE MARCUS (126): Spent childhood in North Carolina, where I entered college at Women's College, University of North Carolina. After a brief and unsuccessful bout with "education" there, I attended Campbell College in Buie's Creek, North Carolina, and Shorter College in Rome, Georgia. Married Warren Marcus after finishing my junior year of college in Rome, and came out here (1954) where I completed my A.B. at San Francisco State. Two children later, I went back to State and got my M.A. Extent of formal education.

Live in San Rafael, California—on a hill which permits privacy—do a lot of staring at the mountain. We have three children now, all girls, ages 14, 12, and 3.

Received a grant from the National Endowment of the Arts in 1968.

Publications: *Motive, Descant, Atlantic Monthly, Poetry Northwest, Red Clay Reader, Southern Poetry Review, Appalachian Review, Massachusetts Review, Cloud Marauder, The*

Living Underground, Tennessee Poetry Journal, Bennington Review, etc.

I'm a part-time instructor at the College of Marin.

Mother, wife, supermarket selector, thing-of-many-parts.

MORTON MARCUS (163): Born New York City 1936. Lived in Bay Area since 1961 (now living in the Santa Cruz mountains). First book: *Origins* (Kayak, 1969). In thirteen anthologies, including *The Young American Poets, Best Poems of 1966, Where is Vietnam?, Poems of War Resistance, The Writer's Mind,* Penguin's *Voices* (England), & *Mixed Bag: Artifacts from the Contemporary Culture.* In sixty or more magazines: *Poetry Northwest, Kayak, Quarterly Review of Literature, Chelsea, Choice, Beloit Poetry Journal, Perspective,* etc.

MICHAEL McCLURE (66): Michael McClure's most recent book of verse was published by Grove Press and is titled *Star.*

JEANNE McGAHEY (50): Born in the coastal hills of Oregon, the timber country where my grandfather was a pioneer, and seeing the big firs disappear mile after mile, I was an early, and futile, protester in the ecology movement. Later I went to Oregon State College, then taught a school with five pupils in an isolated section

of the Oregon sand dunes country.

Winning a copy-writing contest I went somewhat reluctantly into advertising; as an eventual result, wrote for six years a weekly historical documentary narrative for radio called the "Yellow Cab Storyteller." I have written two children's books, *Scareboy* and *Gloomy Erasmus,* a number of magazine articles, and of course as much poetry as time would let me.

Since the mid-thirties I have worked with a group of impressively talented poets (the so-called Activist movement) founded and directed by Lawrence Hart, to whom I have been married since 1944. We now live in Marin County.

In 1941 I was one of New Directions' Five American Poets with Karl Shapiro and three other poets, and have had a pretty wide publication in American and international magazines — both poetry and critical articles. A volume of mine is at present under way at Woolmer/Brotherson, New York.

VINCENT McHUGH (34): Born Providence, Rhode Island, December 23, 1904. Schools: La Salle Academy, 1922; Providence College, ex-1927. Books, all published in the U.S.: five novels—*Touch Me Not* (1930); *Sing Before Breakfast* (1933); *Caleb Catlum's America* (1936); *I Am Thinking of My Darling* (1943); *The Victory* (1947). Short stories: *Edge of the*

World (1953). Poems: *The Blue Hen's Chickens* (1947); *Alpha: The Mutabilities* (1957) (?). Nonfiction: *Primer of the Novel* (1950). Translations (with C. H. Kwock): *Why·I Live on the Mountain* (1958); *The Hermit and the Lady* (1962). Work included in: Federal Writers Project *New York Panorama* and *New York City Guide;* Clifton Fadiman's *Reading I've Liked; Writers of Our Years,* etc. Has contributed to: *New Yorker, Nation, New Republic, Atlantic, Saturday Review, Holiday, Venture,* etc.

Served some twenty years in New York City (1928–1948). After several years in Denver, I lived·in San Francisco from 1952 to 1965. There I worked as a street photographer, organized (with Weldon Kees, Michael Grieg, William Heick and others) a motion-picture company called San Francisco Films, and for a while taught the advanced poetry class at San Francisco State. I was given a $1,000 award by the National Institute of Arts and Letters and (with C. H. Kwock) a $4,000 grant for translation of Chinese poetry by the National Translation Center. I now teach English one afternoon a week in Chinatown, San Francisco, and otherwise largely make a living writing travel articles for *Holiday* and *Venture.*

DAVID MELTZER (22): Poetry: *Ragas* (Discovery Books, S.F., 1959); *The Clown* (Semina, Larkspur, 1960); *The Process* (Oyez, Berkeley, 1965); *The Dark Continent* (Oyez, 1967); *Round the Poem Box* (Black Sparrow Press, L.A. 1969); *From Eden Book* (Maya, S.F., 1969); *Greenspeech* (Christopher Books, Santa Barbara, 1969); *Yesod* (Trigram, London, 1969); & *Luna* (Black Sparrow Press, 1970). Essays: *We All Have Something to Say to Each Other* (Auerhahn Press, S.F., 1962); *Bazascope Mother* (Dreckfesser Press, L.A., 1964); *Journal of the Birth* (Oyez, 1967); *Isla Vista Notes* (Christopher Books, 1970). Fiction: *The Agency Trilogy* (Essex House, L.A., 1968–9); *Orf* (Essex, 1969); *The Martyr* (Essex, 1968); *Brain-Plant Tetralogy* (Essex, 1969). Recordings: *The Serpent Power* (Vanguard, 1968); *Poet Song* (Vanguard, 1969).

JOSEPHINE MILES (12): Born in 1911 in Chicago, Josephine Miles wrote her first poem in 1919 on the kitchen table in joy at the armistice and the end of war. Ever since, she has thought of poems at celebrations, brief moments of joyful amazement at unexpected turns of events or people. She teaches language and literature at Berkeley, and has published volumes of poetry and literary history, the latest being *Kinds of Affection* (Wesleyan, 1967) and *Style and Proportion* (Little, Brown, 1967).

WAYNE MILLER (49): Born September 17, 1939, California. B.F.A. from the San Francisco Art Institute 1966. Worked as farm laborer, carpenter, house painter, mural painter, art reviewer for *Craft Horizons,* staff artist and writer for *Young Hawaii* in Honolulu, editor of *Vision* magazine, taught Francisco State College, guest lecturer in Contemporary Poetry at the San Francisco Art Institute.

Believe poetry should be taken out to the people, the colleges, the neighborhoods, someone's living room, back yard, and in the libraries of their bathrooms. Not only on the podiums, but in the streets.

JANICE MIRIKITANI (111) is the editor of *Aion,* a new Asian-American magazine.

JOSÉ MONTOYA (81): Born in Escabosa, New Mexico, in 1932. Spent early childhood in Sandia and Manzano mountain regions of New Mexico. Moved to barrios of Martinez, Santa Barbara, and San Jose.

In 1942 family moved to Delano, California. Shined shoes and ran errands for prostitutes. From Delano began the farm worker experiences that carried Montoya from the Imperial Valley to the Oregon border. He claims Fowler his California home.

After four years at sea Montoya went to San Diego City College, then on to California College of Arts and Crafts in Oakland. He is presently a professor of art at Sacramento State College.

DANIEL MOORE (165): Born July 30, 1940, 5:20 a.m., Alameda, California. Growing up and school in Oakland, Berkeley, Mexico City, San Francisco. Personal epic *Dawn Visions* written in Mexico and purple San Francisco apartment in 1962, published by City Lights. Manuscripts piled up thru travels and flights, painted books, zazen with Master Suzuki, those golden quiet afternoons! Boston bricks peripheried my vision in 1965 for a year Romance, then return to a dark time finally to Mexico and car-crash, two months flat-on-back monastery. Return to Berkeley to create and direct the Floating Lotus Magic Opera Company for visceral manifestation and expansion of poetic vision for human figures and real voices and orchestra, torchlighting nights open with the dance-rhythm'd Word. Now momentarily dissolved, the Floating Lotus enters the Invisible. It curls up thru your chair. At present writing *States of Amazement.*

Published Work: *Dawn Visions* (City Lights Books, S.F., 1964); *This Body of Black Light Gone Thru the Diamond* (limited ed., 1965). Unpublished Work: *Chants for the Beauty Feast; Vortex; The Rose That Is; The Shark; On the Streets at Night Alone;* *Floating Lotus Notebooks; States of Amazement.*

ROSALIE MOORE (BROWN) (55): Born Oct. 8, in Oakland; school in Alameda and Berkeley . . . University of California, B. A. '32, M. A. '34 . . . but I feel I did my main learning with Lawrence Hart as a long-time associate of the Activist group of poets.

Married Bill Brown, writer and Ranger with State Div. of Beaches and Parks, in 1942, collaborated on ten children's books (Coward-McCann) 1945–1960. Our three daughters: Deborah Turrietta, Celia Barrett, and Camas Brown. Bill died in 1964.

My poems were collected *(The Grasshopper's Man & Other Poems)* by Yale Press in the Yale Poets' Series, 1949, with an introduction by W. H. Auden. Guggenheim Fellowships in creative writing, 1951, 1952. Poems in many magazines and anthologies; most recent publication in *Poetry, Works, Red Clay,* and *Chicago Tribune;* most recently completed long work is a verse play: *The Calydonian Boar Hunt.*

Currently I am teaching at College of Marin, Kentfield, in the Communications Department.

NORMAN OGUE MUSTILL (77): Born 1931, Montreal, Canada; residing in San Anselmo, California. Books: *Fly-paper* (Beach Books, N.Y., 1967), *Twinpak* (Nova Broadcast Press, S.F., 1969), *Mess Kit* (Nova Broadcast Press, S.F. 1970). Coeditor: *VDRSVP* (newspaper, S.F., 1969 –). Works published in: *Express Times, Opus International, The San Francisco Earthquake, Nexus, New Directions, Bulletin From Nothing, Now Now, Kaleidoscope,* etc. Exhibitions in San Francisco, Paris, Heidelberg, Resistencia (Argentina), and Madrid, 1967–70.

LEONARD NATHAN (37): – in all his self-consciousness on himself, and with only a few of the usual kind of "objective" data, such as the fact that he was born in 1924, is married, with three kids, teaches, and has done four books of poems, not counting a few he's finishing up now. These obviously bear on what follows, as did a stay in India a few years ago: that taught him how American he was after all. The forty-five year old, married, fatherly, pedantic, India-travelled Leonard Nathan tries to pay close attention to his own work, which is mainly lyric meditation recently become more and more given over to a highly unserious strain of raffish mocking. He has, with age, become simpler and less lofty. Nevertheless – he hates to see poetry get narrowed down to three fashions, he hates to see sloppiness pass for experiment, and he will, I guess, go on plugging away at his own work which, though he may think it's going to sound like one of the current bright stars, always

182

ends up sounding like him. . . . He tries more and more to cut and trim, believing that silence is a word's best friend, if it is serious. He thinks you can give up pentameters and rhyme (at some cost), but not good structure. No good poem, he mutters to himself, comes in pieces. And as to all the masterpieces written every day by all the master poets, he likes to remember Robert Grave's little caution to the effect that there are many great poems, few good ones.

Needless to say, he is very unhappy with what I have written about him. (*Carol Nathan*)

GEORGE OPPEN (136): *Discrete Series,* with introduction by Ezra Pound (Objectivist Press, 1934); *The Materials* (New Directions/*San Francisco Review,* 1963); *This in Which* (New Directions / *San Francisco Review,* 1965); *Of Being Numerous* (New Directions, 1968).

FRED OSTRANDER (52): Among the sham, the mistakes and the accidents that we seem to be always lost in, poetry can identify a valid moment. I like those who are unafraid to reach out for ways to match words to the thing that has to be said, for ways to identify the moment, even if they are clumsy in doing it . . . .

I have been associated with the Activist group of poets for the past several years. I have appeared in magazines including *Ishmael, Works,* and in the anthology *Accent on Barlow,* and have given several readings with others of the Activist group throughout the Bay Area.

Often it is in the writing of the poem that I think I discover the content, what it was all along that I wanted to say. Because as you work for more and more clarity in the language the event or feelings, the subject of the poem, becomes itself clear.

ANTHONY OSTROFF (99): What would I remember, in a paragraph? World War II (Army). Building our house from the ground up, stick by stick, high in the Berkeley hills. A decade of anti-war activity. Teaching. Writing. Wife and son. And maybe somewhere, way before all that, time in steel mills and factories, hopping freights, playing piano in low dives. No doubt Europe, Canada, Mexico. And certainly this recent span with the Establishment, ending soon for what I would *have* remembered: books remaining to be completed. (Which is not to repudiate books done.)

Publications: 3 *Self Evaluations,* with Galway Kinnel and Winfield Townley Scott (Beloit, 1953); *Imperatives* (Harcourt, Brace & World, 1962); ed., *The Contemporary Poet as Artist and Critic* (Little, Brown, 1964). And some hundred fifty poems, stories, and articles in a variety of places.

PATRICIA A. PARKER (166): I was born, released 26 years ago in a giant vacuum called Texas. In my teens I started writing short stories and continued to do so until 1962 when I married a prose writer and decided that one prose writer in the family was enough. I later decided that that marriage was enough and subsequently remarried, to a poet, of course. I finally figured out that I was not willing to commit myself to marriage and the compromises it entails. Since that time I have been writing both poetry and prose and involving myself in various activities and life styles such as: poetry readings, wrecking sports cars, riding motorcycles, and revolutionary politics.

I believe that a writer should be a mirror not only of her/his personal life but also of the times; therefore any subject from washing dishes to the president can be written about. I dislike "schools of writing" and pedantic labeling, i.e., "academic, romantic, black mountain, beat, imagist, satirist, black, woman, black woman, etc. If a person can't figure out where I'm coming from after reading my work, then either I've failed or they've failed and definitions of me are unimportant.

THOMAS PARKINSON (138) is Professor of English at Berkeley. He has written two books on Yeats and five books of his own poetry. He has edited a casebook on the Beat and a collection of essays on Robert Lowell. He has taught at Bordeaux, Toulouse, Grenoble, Nice, Frankfurt, York, and Oxford. His most recent books are *Protect the Earth* and *Homage to Jack Spicer.* He has just completed two plays that are being produced at Oxford and Berkeley, and he is currently writing a book on Ezra Pound and the Visual Arts and working on a new collection of lyric poems.

CLAUDE PÉLIEU (85): *Le Journal Blanc du Hasard, Embruns d'Exil Traduit du Silence, Les Transistors de l'Innocence* (Christian Bourgois, Paris); *Cahiers de l'Herne & Ecritures des Vivants* (Le Soleil Noir, Paris); in English, from Beach Books/Texts and Documents, N.Y.: *Opal-USA & So Who Owns Death TV?*; forthcoming from City Lights Books: *Letters From The Chelsea.*

ROBERT PETERSON (17): Of Welsh descent, Robert Peterson arrived in San Francisco from Leadville, Colorado, about 1928 and took up residence in a Geary Street hotel one block from Union Square. His early education was in preparation for a career in medicine, but eventually he decided instead to become a teacher. At San Francisco State College, in 1956, he published

his first poem and decided instead to become a poet. At present he is teaching Creative Writing at Reed College.

"I'm not a 'natural' — I'm always worrying it; especially because I want a poem to seem easy, unemcumbered, and inevitable — like the way a mind *ought* to work. I'm indecisive, unwise, nervous, and gamble a lot. I may start with an old jacknife, a model airplane, a green surgeon's gown, a couple of white mice and some random notes on thrift. From things like this I try to cut a suit that fits."

In 1965, he published *Vietnam Blues,* the first American anthology of Vietnam protest poems. His most recent book is *Wondering Where You Are* (Kayak Press, 1969). His home is in Mill Valley, California.

CHARLES PLYMELL (46) was born in Holcomb, Kansas, 1935. He is of Cherokee Indian, Welsh, English, and Scotch descent. He grew up on a farm on the plains of Kansas and attended school in Wichita. He then drifted working on farms and ranches in the Dakotas, Texas, Wyoming. He rode in rodeos in Arizona, worked in an auto daredevil show in Oklahoma. Followed work on pipelines, New Mexico, Arizona; California, catskinner; Colorado, truck driver; Alaska. Travelled in Mexico. Worked on the railroad. Worked a steamdrill building The Dalles Dam, Columbia River, Washington-Oregon.

Became a printer and settled in San Francisco. Met the poets of the Beat Generation. Lived with the late Neal Cassidy ("Dean Moriarty" in *On the Road*) and Allen Ginsberg in an old Victorian flat in San Francisco. Helped spawn the Hippy Generation or the Now Generation. Saw the Haight Ashbury come and go. Got fed up with the whole psychedelic scene. Married Pamela Beach in Reno, Nevada. Travelled to Europe, came back and went to work on the docks in San Francisco as a teamster. Then to Baltimore where he has been working on his M.A. at Johns Hopkins University, writing a novel and playing with his new-born daughter.

Books: *Apocalypse Rose* (Dave Haselwood Books, San Francisco, 1966); *Neon Poems* (Atom Mind Publications, Syracuse, N.Y., 1970); *Cherokee* (Christian Bourgois, *ed.*, Paris, 1970). Periodicals: *Weapon, Long Hair* (London), *Akzente* (Germany), *Poetry* (Chicago); *City Lights Journal* (San Francisco), *Evergreen Review, Nola Express, The San Francisco Earthquake, Paris Review,* etc.

ISHMAEL REED (74): Novelist and poet; born in Tennessee in 1938; now in Berkeley. Novel: *The Free-Lance Pallbearers* (Doubleday, 1967). *(ed.)*

KENNETH REXROTH (130): Born in 1905, Kenneth Rexroth has long been a central part of the San Francisco literary scene. The essential poetry of most major languages and traditions has been his campanion and sure educatrix since his youth, and the vigorous example of his life and work has quickened the creative work of several generations around him. He now lives at home with his family in Santa Barbara. (*ed.*)

STAN RICE (116): I was born of lower-middle class white parents in Dallas, Texas, in 1942. The problems, the things I must overcome to tell my most courageous truths are not what a ghetto black must overcome. I was an excellent student, newspaper editor, National Honor Society member, etc. I can make words glitter and crackle, I can juggle language and "create" a sparkling artifact which is totally irrelevant to human experience. I must constantly work *against* my ability to make glassy artifacts. Some of my poems perhaps reflect this struggle. What saves me is an aspect of Southern Protestanism which is seldom discussed: its tendency to launch a child into a definitionless Void in which anything can happen and the individual will is the only limit. I grew up with no knowledge of the cultural richness of being Catholic or Jewish or Black. The matrix was neutral. No books in the house, no prejudices about books. Truckers and painters can develop in such an environment with almost equal ease. I learned early to celebrate the "sensuality" of life's largeness. This led to a corresponding dumbness in terms of subtly, analytic accuracy, understanding of motivation, some of the more respected values in poetry from a literary standpoint. What I love most to do is *read* my poems. I must always be careful to keep a poem from being so much of a musical score for spoken voice that it loses its on-the-page life. This is a big problem. If the poem becomes too much of a musical score it can look "stagey" or artificial on the page. Its rhythms get too slippery. But the act of reading is the whole and final emotional consummation of the poem for me. I always write with an image in my head of the psychology of the Voice that would speak this poem. When I read the poem aloud I pay attention to the words and try to read the poem as it wants to be read. My only godform is Energy. I like a poem that is sensual and large and spread out and full of imagery mixed with naturalistic language and one that does a lot of things and that is physically exciting to read aloud. In the context of this superfluity I strive also for a tightness and economy of language, making each word feel like it really should be in the poem . . . a ferocious lucidity. I live in Berkeley with my wife Anne (a novelist) and four year old daughter. I teach creative writing at San Francisco State College where I'm the Assistant Director of the Poetry Center.

EUGENE RUGGLES (40): Born Dec. 4, 1936, Pontiac, Michigan; attended Northern Michigan and Wayne State Universities. Have worked as a hospital orderly, gardener, fireman on the Southern Pacific Railroad, and merchant seaman, among others.

Instead of their influence, I would say I have *loved* the poems of Whitman, Lawrence, Thomas, Crane, Jeffers, Roethke, Stafford, Wright, Kinnell. . . .

Poems published in *Chelsea, Kayak, Poetry Northwest, Poetry* (Chicago), *Sumac, The Nation, Minnesota Review, Choice,* and in the anthology *60 on the 60's.* Recently received a $3,000 grant from the National Endowment for the Arts. Presently living on a sheep ranch near Bodega Bay, California.

As for poetics: poetry is my life. That's all. Next comes man. And then God. Though I'm never sure when that order has been changed. For instance, I truly feel that Chavez has more poetry in his life than four-fifths of all the so-called poets in our nation — and that the Indians on Alcatraz are closer to poetry than *Poetry,* Chicago. They and Chavez both have a vision.

If it doesn't want to become as dead as politics, as dead as most of this society, poetry must love its way back into the blood of the people. And the earth. 185

It has to give itself over to the awful human problems that are destroying us, and to reach *inward* to a true spiritual level. American poetry has seldom done either. It is not doing them today.

Anyway, regardless of what happens — I'm probably one of the luckiest men alive.

DAVID SCHAFF (143) was born in Philadelphia, 16 February 1943. Convinced a bit about poetry at Yale, later edited "New American Poetry" issues of *The Yale Literary Magazine*, 1963 & –5. Migrated to San Francisco in June 1965. Put together an occasional magazine, *Ephemeris*, and two published books, *Tables* (1966) and *The Ladder* (1967); another, *The Moon by Day*, due from Four Seasons soon. Various projects, articles and broadsides. At present engaged in Art History program at the University of California, Berkeley. Not for long. Interested in music, vision, birds, conservation. *Light Poems*.

JAMES SCHEVILL (71): Born in Berkeley, California, 1920. Graduated from Harvard University, 1942. Army 1942–6. Has taught at the California College of Arts and Crafts, San Francisco State College (Director of the Poetry Center 1961–7), and is currently Professor of English at Brown University. Married and the father of two children. Plays have been performed widely throughout the United States, in England, and in Holland. Has given many readings from his poems and plays. Recently, he has been concerned with experimental performing poems. His books include: *Private Dooms & Public Destinations: Poems 1945–1962; The Stalingrad Elegies; Violence & Glory: Poems 1962–1968;* and *The Black President & Other Plays,* all published by Swallow Press, Inc. Forthcoming: a new play, *Lovecraft's Follies,* scheduled for 1970.

NINA SERRANO (107): I was born in New York City in 1934 and began writing in 1968 during a four-month's stay in Cuba as part of a film unit. The energy of the Cuban Revolution and the perfumed tropical air moved me to write poems, movies and articles.

JOHN OLIVER SIMON (152): Born 1942. Dances in heavy boots. Learning to be father; learning hopefully not too late. Books: *Roads to Dawn Lake, Dancing Bear,* two others, new due from Oyez. Edits *Aldebaran Review.* (*Alta Simon*)

PATRICK SMITH (112): I'm from Menominee, Michigan, nearly forty. I live with a beautiful woman, and our seven beautiful children. I teach in a small, private university, make films when I can, and write. I have been in San Francisco for about five years, and consider it my home town. Almost all my poetry has been written since I came here.

GARY SNYDER (33) was born in San Francisco, reared in Seattle, educated in Portland, Bloomington, Berkeley, San Francisco, and Kyoto. He says, "My poetic mentors are: Tu Fu, Archilochus, Rexroth, Duncan, Milarepa, Buson, Blake, Lawrence, Jeffers, Whitman, Pound, Williams, Whalen, (and Graves, but not as a poet). I've got one more: the People (ancient Singers of Turtle Island, and the unknown Makers of devotional Tantric songs)." He is finishing building a house in the Sierra foothills and hopes to soon resume work on *Mountains and Rivers Without End,* and commence a series of hymns to logic and ecstacy in their play with the interrelatedness of myriad phenomena.

GEORGE STANLEY (149), male, white, native of S.F. (therefore "American," i.e., U.S. citizen), middle-class, Irish Catholic. Homosexual? A poet. ("Identity . . . *what one is never not*" — Erik H. Erikson.) When I was 23 I felt 73 at heart. Now, at 36 I am just about 27. Horizons of language and love that stretch out wider than I had ever thought. Politics and society still scare me (police, youth haters, paranoids, order-followers, entropy) but I am not so scared this year as I was last.

We are a social animal. Love or starve (Middle English for die). I have abandoned the pose of "existentialism" — spiritual privatization — but still wear the black turtleneck sweater (as an emblem of something else I can never not be, a beatnik?). When I was 22 at the University of California, Berkeley, I thought all I would ever need or want in life would be my FM radio and sherry. (And, sometimes, I still feel that way, but more, I love men, women, boys, cooking, the country, drugs, other poets' poetry (like Wyatt, Baudelaire), sex, chess, wine, talk, dreams, am into my own next poem, want to go to Dublin, want to go to India . . . .) When I die I hope that experience will not be just like going to sleep, but I'm afraid it might be — then I think, gee, maybe that blank is just a false image I ought to attribute to my socialization.

LYNN STRONGIN (30): I was born and raised in New York City. My early studies were in musical composition. I took a B.A. at Hunter College, then came to the West Coast about seven years ago to take an M.A. in English at Stanford. I have taught college since then: Long Island University, Merritt College, and most recently at Mills College in Oakland. Publication in: *Trace, Sumac, The Ladder, Motive, Man-Root,* etc., and in the anthologies *31 New American Poets* (Hill & Wang, 1970), *American Literary An-*thology 3 (Viking, 1970), and in the forthcoming *Sisterhood Is Powerful* (Random House), *Green Flag* (City Lights), & *The New Women* (Bobbs-Merrill). Also forthcoming: *The Rose Poems—A Trilogy* (Oyez, 1970).

KATHLEEN TEAGUE (82): The poet prefers her biographical background to remain anonymous.

SOTÈRE TORREGIAN (159): Born 1941, of Afro and Arab ancestry. Raised in Newark, New Jersey, where attended Rutgers University. Associated with "New York Group" of poets and painters in New York City 1962–. Removed to California 1966–7. Received the Poets Foundation Award for Poetry in 1967–8. Anthologies: *The Young American Poets* (Follett, 1968); *New Black Voices* (1970). Books: *The Wounded Mattress* (Oyez, Berkeley, 1965); *Song for Woman* (first issued in N.Y. in 1965; now being expanded and re-issued); in preparation: *The Age of Gold,* poems 1968–70. Frequent contributor to: *Paris Review, Art and Literature* (Paris, now defunct); *The World* (N.Y.), etc. At present an instructor and writer-in-residence in Afro-American Studies at Stanford University.

CHARLES UPTON (87): Every time I write an autobiography, I see that my whole life has changed, my whole Past. Every new petal that unfolds, old limb that drops off changes the whole thing, all the way back to birth & beyond. This leads me to suspect that nothing ever really happened. Leads me to suspect we are all in Eternity, as has been reported by reliable sources. I was born in San Francisco, December 13, 1948, the story says. Raised in San Rafael. Never went to college. Wrote a lot. Traveled in U.S., Mexico, Canada. Hitchhiked. Hopped freights. Took drugs. Led a normal life. When I pick a flower, I find that everything that has ever happened, all the power of the Universe, stars crashing & boiling nebulae, has conspired & moved through my hand that I break the stem in one certain way. This is Magik. Should I therefore have a feeling of power? Should I stare hard?

NANOS VALAORITIS (78): Born in Lausanne, Switzerland, of Greek parents, studied Classics and Law in the University of Athens and Languages in the University of London and the Sorbonne. Valaoritis, a poet of Surrealist tendency, has been associated with the Parisian avant-garde where he had a play produced by Marc'O. Another play of his was produced by Giancarlo Menotti in Spoleto and again in Aarhus, Denmark, by the students. He has also done object assemblages and collages. From 1963 until the year of the Coup in Greece, 1967, he edited the

187

review *Pali,* which represented the most vital and experimental side of Greek writing and painting. Today this group, one member of which commited suicide after the Coup, is scattered in many countries. All are doing well and represent the upcoming generation of Greek writers and poets. Both those who have remained in Greece and those who have left are preparing a comeback with protest literature of resistance against the regime.

Valaoritis' work, due to many displacements and to living in different countries, is scattered in magazines such as *Folio, Botteghe Oscure, Horizon, Encounter, London Magazine, Vindrosen* (Denmark), *Lettres Nouvelles* (France), *Poetry* (Chicago), *Kayak,* and *Antinarcissus.* In Greek he has published two volumes of verse: *Punishment of the Magicians* (1947), *Central Arcade* (1958); and in French, *Terre de Diamant,* with drawings by his wife Marie Wilson, through whom he met André Breton and the Surrealists in 1954. This meeting was of capital importance to him, since it saved him from cynicism, despair, and Literature with a capital L. He has also translated many Greek poets, among whom he prefers the great Greek Surrealist and psychoanalyst Andreas Embirikos, and the painter and Surrealist poet Nikos Engonopoulos.

He is now teaching at the State College of San Francisco, where he finds himself very much at home among the faculty and the students.

Two new books of poems are in preparation: *Hypnotic Pencils* and *Birds of Hazard and Prey,* from which the poem in this volume has been selected.

LEWIS WARSH (115) was born November 9, 1944, in New York City. He graduated from The Bronx High School of Science (1961) & from City College of New York (1966). Edited *Angel Hair* magazine & books with Anne Waldman (1966–1970). His poems & reviews have appeared in the following publications: *Adventures in Poetry, Best & Co., The Floating Bear, Art & Literature, Wild Dog, The Paris Review, The Ant's Forefoot, Caterpillar, Poetry, The Young American Writers, The World Anthology,* etc. Toad Press, in Eugene, Oregon, published his first book: *The Suicide Rates,* a long poem written in 1963. The book appeared in 1967. In 1968: *Moving Through Air* (Angel Hair Books) & *Highjacking* (Boke Press) appeared, and in 1969 *Chicago,* 5 poems written with Tom Clark, was published by Angel Hair. Visited Bolinas, California, August 1968; returned October 1969.

RUTH WEISS (62): Born Berlin 1928. Shoved to Vienna 1933. Found home San Francisco 1952 via Quaker Iowa Chicago cement New Orleans. Crawled to a Los Angeles hill 1967 where *Desert Journal,* a seven-year work was completed. 1970 back to San Francisco. Books: *Steps* (1958); *Gallery of Women* (1959); *South Pacific* (1959); *Blue in Green* (1960). Magazines: *Beatitude, New Orleans Quarterly, Gallery Sail, Sun Nightshade, Film Culture, Semina, Outburst, Matrix.* Film: *The Brink,* 40 min. film poem (1961). Has written 12 plays, all one-acts.

LEW WELCH (64), one of the survivors of the Beat Generation, is currently living in Marin County, writing and teaching. He makes his living working on the docks of San Francisco as a longshoreman-clerk. He got his B.A. at Reed College, where he roomed with Gary Snyder and Philip Whalen, lifelong friends and accomplices. He is known for his powerful readings and has published: *Wobbly Rock, On Out, Courses, The Song Mt. Tamalpais Sings,* and innumerable pieces in little magazines and in the form of broadsides. His collected works, *Ring of Bone,* will appear sometime in 1971, published either by Grove Press or in the Writing series of Don Allen's Four Seasons Press.

JOHN WIENERS (92) is a graduate of Boston College in Massachusetts, a student of Charles Olson at Black Mountain College and a candidate for a Masters degree in Humanities at the State University of New York at Buffalo, New York. He is a bachelor in his midthirties and a contributing editor to *Anonym* magazine. San Francisco was his home from 1957 to 1960, and then New York during the early and midsixties. He is the recipient of Annual Literary Awards in 1967 and 1968, and has read since at Boston University, the University of Massachusetts, and at St. Mark's Church in New York City. He lives outside Boston with his widowed father and his regular friends are Gerret Lansing, Gerard Malanga and Edward Dorn. He is under contract to Jonathan Cape, Ltd., London.

PETE WINSLOW (144): Born Oct. 19, 1934, in Seattle, grad of University of Washington where I edited a humor magazine, made a living as a newspaperman since 1956, turned on by Ginsberg 1957 and Lamantia 1967, now surrealist, married, one child. Writings: *Whatever Happened to Pete Winslow* (1960) and *The Rapist and Other Poems* (1962), both out of print; *Monster Cookies* (1967), in print and available from me; *Mount Gogo* (novel, 1968) and *Mummy Tapes* (1970), both unpublished. Current project: essays on contemporary poetry.

AL YOUNG (15): Grew up in Mississippi & Detroit. Came of age in the Bay Area. Wrote stories & voice plays (cowboy, detective, life on other planets) in grade school. Began writing poems in junior high, turned on by Black music, the way people around me talked & sang, Li Po & Patchen. Earned a little money singing myself but also worked at a hundred other gigs. Once even played the youthful Archie Moore, the boxer, in a documentary TV film written by San Francisco novelist Frank Chin. Founded & edit the occasional *Loveletter*. Write novels (*Snakes; Who is Angelina?*) as well as books of poetry (*Dancing; The Song Turning Back Into Itself*). Poetry, when it's for real, whisks me up out of my momentary self & puts me in intimate touch with everything at the same time. It's a part of my religion.